Praise for *The EduProtocol Field Guide*

"This is the book I've heard teachers begging for without realizing it. Everywhere I work with teachers, they talk about time being their biggest hurdle to accomplishing their goals and dreams in the classroom. *The EduProtocol Field Guide* helps them buy that time back because they don't have to reinvent the wheel every time they lesson plan. Any teacher can use the examples in this book to create more engaging classes in less time, freeing them up to be uniquely themselves and develop relationships with students."

—Matt Miller, educator, blogger, speaker, and author of *Ditch That Textbook* and coauthor of *Ditch That Homework*

"One of the most practical books I've read in a long time, *The EduProtocol Field Guide* provides structure and format, empowering educators to maintain a laser-like focus on teaching and learning and the individual needs of each student. Hebern and Corippo will undoubtedly make you laugh—while simultaneously tapping emotion—as they share their real-world stories from decades of classroom experience. This book is not simply one you read; it's one that you use, and then use again! *The EduProtocol Field Guide* is undoubtedly a must-read for teachers of all skill levels looking to amplify the student-learning experience through the effective use of technology."

—Thomas C. Murray, director of innovation, Future Ready Schools, Washington, DC

"This book should be given to every pre-service and current instructor as the Bible for great teaching. Not only will these EduProtocols engage students and improve learning, they will also ease the daily workload for teachers. Stop carrying those totes of worksheets and essays home. This book is going to change your teaching and learning forever."

—Lisa DeLapo, innovator in residence, Krause Center for Innovation and director, KCI MERIT Program

"*The EduProtocol Field Guide* is a valuable resource for creative instructional strategies that will make teaching any academic content active, engaging, and enriching. Marlena Hebern and Jon Corippo are your friendly neighborhood education coaches prepping you with practical insights drawn from years of experience as classroom teachers and education leaders. Good humor and banter set the tone for how teachers can transform a regular lesson into a dynamic student-centered learning experience. Their stories and anecdotes are relevant and will make you laugh and warm your heart. The critical takeaway is that EduProtocols and Smart Start strategies lead teachers to creatively teach with greater time efficiency and fantastic effectiveness and helping students reach mastery. That only lea   in learning will

                                                     r,
DivergentED Consultants

"It won't be long before EduProtocol Field Guide is required reading in all teacher credential programs! It is the essential, simple guide to planning a perfect week and repeating it thirty-two times! The protocols are straightforward and captivating lesson shells integrated with technology to engage students in the Four Cs (critical thinking, communication, collaboration, and creativity). The EduProtocols combined with the Smart Start Activities are a must for all teachers wanting to establish a routine that builds positive culture and relationships in the classroom while delivering curriculum in an engaging and targeted manner."

–Diana Dietz, new teacher induction mentor/coach, Atwater Elementary School District, Atwater, CA

"If someone suggested an approach to your teaching that would allow you to make what you do both less cumbersome for you and more effective for your students, would you try it? In *The EduProtocol Field Guide*, Hebern and Corippo work to show how teachers can help students focus on the content rather than the tasks that make up each day's class, with the personal and professional benefits that come from raising one's game as a thoughtful educator.

"It's no small conceptual leap to take the variety of activities one uses, shine a bright light on them, and ask honestly how well they work. This book, though, provides a path for creating intellectually meaningful systems that become familiar to students for exploring content, and explains how doing so can make for more efficient use of time and energy on the part of the teacher.

"The chapters include suggestions for starters and protocols designed to get students into a frame of mind that allows for deeper learning while getting teachers focused on being the kind of guide whom students trust to help them explore the unknown and believe in their ability to do so.

"The authors regularly return to practical questions of what it means to become better as a teacher. In particular, they talk about "more reps" to encourage teachers not to lose heart as they seek to bring a new technique to their work—practice makes one better, after all, and our following that message (one we so regularly give our students) is at the core of the guidance we get in the book.

"This is a great read for teachers and an especially strong book for those tasked with helping teachers develop professionally."

–Rushton Hurley, founder and executive director, NextVista.org

"Protocols have changed my teaching style and effectiveness such that I actually enjoy planning, instruction, and the work that goes along with it. I have exponentially more time on my hands because I use protocols. Additionally, our classroom culture is infinitely better, and I am less stressed. All in all, I can't say enough about the value of what I've learned from Jon and Marlena."

–Nate Shankles, advisor, staff internship coordinator, social science teacher, Big Picture High School, Fresno, CA

Bring Your Teaching into Focus

EduProtocol
FIELD GUIDE

— 16 —

Student-Centered Lesson Frames

for Infinite Learning Possibilities

Marlena Hebern & Jon Corippo

The EduProtocol Field Guide

© 2018 by Marlena Hebern and Jon Corippo

This book is available at special discounts when purchased in quantity for use as premiums, promotions, fundraisers, or for educational use. For inquiries and details, contact the publisher at books@daveburgessconsulting.com.

Published by Dave Burgess Consulting, Inc.
San Diego, CA
DaveBurgessConsulting.com

Cover Design by Genesis Kohler
Editing and Interior Design by My Writers' Connection

Library of Congress Control Number: 2018932043
Paperback ISBN: 978-1-946444-60-8
Ebook ISBN: 978-1-946444-62-2
First Printing: March 2018

Contents

Comprehensive Chart
of Smart Starts and EduProtocols

EduProtocol	Smart Start	Protocol	Game	Activity	Un-Plugged Option	Slides	Students Present
Cardboard Challenge	✓			✓			✓
Cat and Dog	✓				✓	✓	
Frayer a Classmate	✓	✓		✓	✓	✓	
Paper Airplane	✓			✓	✓		
Things That Rock	✓			✓			
Worst Preso Ever	✓					✓	✓
BookaKucha		✓				✓	✓
Cyber Sandwich		✓				✓	
Digital Class Book		✓				✓	✓
Fast and the Curious		✓					
Frayer		✓			✓	✓	
Great American Race		✓	✓			✓	
Group Brainstorm		✓				✓	
Internet Scavenger Hunt		✓	✓			✓	
Iron Chef		✓				✓	✓
Learning in the Round		✓			✓		
Math Reps		✓			✓	✓	
Mini-Report		✓			✓		
Primary-Source		✓				✓	✓
Tech Coach		✓				✓	
3-Act Math®		✓			✓		
8 p*ARTS		✓			✓		

Foreword
By Alice Keeler

My teacher-prep program left me woefully unprepared to be in a classroom with real students. Sure, I learned the six steps to writing a lesson plan, but I didn't learn how to create *engaging* lessons. I took to heart the advice about being nice to the secretaries (because they control, well, everything), but my studies failed to cover how to *build a classroom culture* that makes students want to learn. My professors encouraged me to make home visits, but they never talked about how to really *listen* to parent concerns and *use that feedback* to change my approach. I learned to rely on rubrics, but none of my teacher-prep classes covered appropriate ways to challenge the status quo. So when I graduated, I had my teaching certificate—and very little understanding of how to actually teach students.

During my first few years as a math teacher, I gave students packets of worksheets—lots of worksheets. A typical class period for me started by spending fifteen minutes going over homework—not exactly a hook into learning. After squandering those valuable first minutes of class and ensuring my students were properly bored, I would write a problem on the board that no one cared about and then follow up by doing the thinking for my students and writing down the procedural steps for the math problem. Then I would wait for students to copy the problem and the steps to solving it. I would then put another math problem on the board and work it out for the students. And, again, I would wait while they copied everything I'd written. After that, we would do some guided practice during which I waited for the students to try a problem, one that I would eventually do for them so they could check their answers. Guided practice continued until the final few minutes of class when students could start on their homework.

I spent so much class time waiting for kids to copy my work when I could have been offering feedback. I did so much thinking for my students when they could have been working through problems together—challenging themselves and one another to try any number of methods for solving problems instead of the one way I presented.

Why did I teach this way? Simple. It's the way I was taught in school. Beyond that, I was following the exact lesson plan examples I had submitted to my professors in my teacher-prep program. Sadly, none of those professors told me how boring those lessons were. Neither did my teachers provide examples of ways to better engage my students; they taught me the way they had learned, and the boring cycle continued. Only, I didn't realize just how boring it was. I loved my subject matter, and I loved talking about it. I thought that if I was having a good time, the students would too.

It's no wonder that when school is portrayed on television shows, it's rarely in a positive light. In fact, school is almost universally depicted by unfunny jokes that hit a little too close to home as they point to and laugh at the classroom as a place that sucks the life out of students. I don't want to be the teacher that is joked about on television. And when I started to hear the murmurings of my disenchanted students, I knew something had to change.

It took time and lots of planning, trial, and error, but I finally discovered ways to make my lessons fun. I discovered ways to ditch homework and keep kids engaged and even excited about learning. How I wish I'd had the tools and insights Jon and Marlena provide in this book. Using the EduProtcols and Smart Starts as the foundation or starting points for lesson planning would have simplified my life and, more importantly, would have made my classroom and lessons more enjoyable—for *everyone*.

The EduProtocol Field Guide offers specific examples for how to engage students in activities that result in learning. These experienced educators challenge us to develop those mindsets that are open to new possibilities for teaching and learning, a practice that's important for you, your students, and the next generation. We are not just teaching this generation but the generation they will teach.

Think about it: It's very likely one of the students in your classroom today will end up being a teacher. What mindsets do you want your students to develop and take forward with them into the classrooms of tomorrow? What do your students currently equate with learning? Do students see school as a stack of paperwork with lines to be filled out? Is class about watching the teacher work? Or is it about discovery and exploration? Might it include using technology to take learning further and make it more personal? And shouldn't it involve building a culture where kids feel cared for, where they are encouraged to communicate, collaborate, create, and to think critically—for the sake of all our futures—to challenge the status quo?

You can teach the way you were taught, or you can choose to teach in a way that doesn't suck the life out your students. Rather than waiting for students to copy vocab, facts, and math problems, use a Smart Start or an EduProtocol to try something new. And if the lesson doesn't go as you'd hoped, tweak things and try again. Jon and Marlena call that "doing reps," and it's how we learn to build better lessons.

No matter your subject area, the EduProtocols and Smart Starts in this book will equip you with powerful and engaging alternatives to the traditional lecture-and-worksheet teaching model. As you read, I'm sure you'll be inspired to put these ideas into practice and give them your own twist. And if you're like me, you'll find yourself thinking, *this book is the teacher-prep program I wish I'd had!*

Alice Keeler

coauthor of *50 Things You Can Do with Google Classroom* and *Ditch That Homework*

I begin with an idea and then it becomes something else.

—Pablo Picasso

HR plopped several résumés on the table. I (Marlena) picked up the stack and flipped through them. *Don't know him, don't know him, don't know her.* Then I recognized a name: Jon Corippo.

I met Jon a few years earlier, around 2006, at some district professional-learning events, but I didn't really know him. In fact, I had stayed away from his group because they were much too techie for me. (If only I'd known.) I skimmed his résumé:

Google Certified Educator. *What was that?*

Apple Distinguished Educator. *So he likes Apple products?*

eighteen years' experience in the classroom. *That's a good number and means he has valuable classroom experience.*

Presented at conferences. *An entire page? Does he ever work?*

YouTube Teacher. *Is there such a thing?*

I then wondered why Jon was looking for a job in my district. Had he been displaced? He seemed like a nice guy. He had a great job at Minarets High School; in fact, his résumé said he was the cofounder of Minarets. Regardless, it was time for the interview.

Jon sat at the end of the crowded table and placed his iPad face down. *Who brings an iPad to an interview?* I'd never heard of such a thing. He glanced around the panel, obviously a little nervous. We listened to Jon answer question after question in quick succession. A stark difference from the previous interviewee who obviously didn't have a clear idea of what this new movement (called "Common Core") was about.

Our last question, a fun one we hoped would bring insight into the thinking of our candidate, was, "Name ten ways to use a pencil." Jon listed ten, and all of them had a curriculum or technology connection, including an app to measure the arc of the pencil if it were thrown. *Hmm, I never would have thought of that one.*

As Jon left the room, it dawned on me: He's going to teach Common Core through technology. Tech isn't a side piece; it is the missing piece! I spent those first two years trying to unlock the "wonders" of Common Core, but I was the only academic coach in my district and had been unable to find its magic. Now, in this moment of revelation, I got it. I immediately saw the power Jon's methodology could bring by leveraging technology as a vehicle to teach content. Simply brilliant. I had to know more.

We hired him.

What followed were two rapid-fire years in which Jon and I, under Jon's leadership, changed our rural district forever. Our department staff consisted of three: Jon, who was hired as the director of curriculum and instruction, myself, a K–8 English language arts teacher on special assignment, and one secretary. The three of us ran all the curriculum, training, technology decisions, purchases, implementation, transitional (Pre-K) kindergarten implementation, textbook purchases and training, district transfers, and duties as assigned for a district of roughly one hundred teachers. And in year two, when our secretary became ill, it was just Jon and me.

In one year, Jon purchased devices, implemented 1:1 in grades six through twelve, reworked all the Wi-Fi hubs in the district, moved Wi-Fi control to a central office, provided training to the IT department, and began a transition to Google Apps for Education. He implemented training for teachers at a ratio of 8:1 (that's eight trainings for each teacher) and introduced our teachers to great minds such as John Stevens, Matt Vaudrey, Dan Meyers, Alice Keeler, Dave Burgess, and a host of other educators from around California who visited to inspire our staff. Jon prepared our district as a Future Ready District and secured an invitation to the White House for his efforts.

It was a whirlwind year.

But it wasn't just our district that changed: I changed.

I had my eye on an administrative position, but I didn't have a very clear vision of my path moving forward. I spent about half of my time writing, copying, distributing, and scoring benchmarks. The other half of my time I spent working with teachers and principals on curriculum goals, training teachers, managing the district's tech programs, and whatever was asked of me.

All that changed when Jon arrived.

I began working more closely with teachers. Then I began presenting at conferences, which was not an easy task since I had developed a fear of speaking to large audiences. The first engagement Jon volunteered me for was a local conference in which I was to be a member of a panel. I managed to get through it despite advancing the slide show in the wrong direction. *Ahhh, the clicker has a top* and *a bottom button.* I'd never used one of those before!

When the discussion finished, I sat at the keynote table next to Alan November, author of *Who Owns the Learning?* and founder of November Learning. I didn't know who Alan was and sent a quick text to Jon to find out. "Hmm . . . a big name," he replied.

I returned to my district with fresh enthusiasm and clear direction for our work.

I was challenged with many tasks, and somehow I was able to navigate them, growing all the while. In that one year, I managed to plan Edcamp Yosemite (a few months earlier, I hadn't known what an Edcamp was), became a Rock Star Faculty member at the Petaluma Rock Star Camp (had never attended one before), presented at Fall CUE and National CUE (despite being very nervous), discovered two thousand other educators on Twitter (wasn't that just a trendy thing?), became a Google Educator (had never used Google prior to that year but passed all five exams in one week after studying like crazy), and completed the Leading Edge Administrator Certification course.

Up until Jon's arrival, the last real professional development (PD) day my district had hosted was about eight years prior, around 2007. That first year was a year of learning and catching up, and I had a lot of catching up to do! I worked hard, and my learning curve has not stopped or slowed down since. The year following Jon's departure, I returned to the classroom, then left for a new job with the Fresno County Superintendent of Schools in central California and became a Google Certified Innovator and a Google Certified Trainer. I now plan professional learning for teachers across the county (and sometimes the state) on engaging students through technology, hands-on tech, and district implementation of technology in the classroom for grades K–12. Last year our department of three coaches impacted more than seven hundred teachers with training and classroom coaching.

I hope the learning curve keeps climbing.

When I started on this pathway, I was an experienced teacher of sixteen years. I had a master's degree in teaching reading and had taught in grades spanning kindergarten to eighth grade. I knew and loved my craft and worked to maximize the limited technology available in my classroom: a microphone, a few web-based programs, and a Promethean board. Looking back, I realize I had the most important requirements: Love kids, love what you do, and desire to be better every day.

My "secrets" for striving to improve are available to everyone:

Be open to possibilities yet unseen.

Try (and break) stuff.

Make your own stuff.

After the second year, Jon left our district to begin work at CUE as the CUE Director of Innovation. (Can you get a cooler title than that?) In his first year, he increased CUE's outreach from 2,500 teachers trained per year to 20,000 per year and growing. Today, he serves as the organization's director.

Beginning in my old district, Jon and I forged a friendship around our work and shared goals for kids. Since then, our journeys have brought us to different places, and despite bringing our respective strengths and views on education to the table, we have one thing in common: We love kids, we love what we do, and we want to be better.

Marlena

Jon, did I steal that from you? Did you say that first?

Jon

It's just the truth, not sure who said it first.

One day, in the fall of 2017, I said to Jon, "I'd like to write a book."

And he replied, "I'd collaborate on that with you."

So here we are, honored and thrilled to share sixteen EduProtocols for putting the power technology into the hands of kids, and six Smart Start Activities to help you launch positive culture in your classroom.

What is Smart Start?

Smart Start is the process of setting aside the curriculum in order to build culture at the beginning of the year. The focus is on teaching kids how to learn, using things like Frayer Models and Venn Diagrams on fun subjects to get then ready for the year. As you scaffold fun into curriculum, students develop a sense of belonging, and you'll find that you'll reap the benefits all year long! The Smart Start EduProtocols begin with Chapter 4.

What are EduProtocols?

EduProtocols are lesson shells into which you insert your curriculum to teach more effectively and deliver more engaging content. We want to see students collaborating, creating, critically thinking, and communicating (the Four Cs), and we want you to know that you can use these ideas to change your classroom! EduProtocols are introduced in Chapter 2 and are explained in detail in beginning with Chapter 15.

Getting Better

The most important part of "getting better" is to start now. Find a practical element you can manage and give it a try. Don't worry about failure; it takes practice (we call these "reps") to develop new skills. And as teachers (just as with kids), our skill set is continually evolving.

That's what this book is about: changing classroom reality in simple, manageable ways to create a meaningful impact on kids.

You can read this book in order from cover to cover and enjoy the insights, stories, and the six Smart Starts and sixteen EduProtocols. Or you might choose to begin by reading just the EduProtocols. Or perhaps you'd like to start with a particular activity to try in your classroom.

Whichever you choose, use this book to bridge the gap between subject matter and delivery with meaningful EduProtocols you create with your content. Smart Start activities and EduProtocols are formatted to get kids collaborating, creating, thinking critically, and communicating. And this book is formatted to help you start planning now. Make notes in the space provided in the margins. We want this guide to be something you refer back to again and again.

This book and its message are a joint effort. As we share personal stories and experiences, we will identify the speaker, but most of the time, what you will see is a united voice regarding the power and simplicity of the Smart Starts and Edu-Protocols we've created and adapted throughout our careers. We hope you find it to be valuable.

We love to hear what teachers are doing and hope you'll share your progress, insights, and the lessons you create!

Connect with us on Twitter:
@mhebern and @jcorippo

Visit our website:
eduprotocols.com

A Note
on Technology Platforms

We use more than one platform to facilitate student collaboration. When we design for kids, we generally use Google, but Microsoft and Apple have developed collaboration features in their programs as well. The activities in this book can be used in any platform that allows for collaboration, even though we originally designed them in Google. In our writing, we are general in specifying the programs used; please refer to your own platform support to learn how to use your collaboration features.

Chapter 1

Creative Learning by Heart

*You can't use up creativity. The more
you use, the more you have.*

—Maya Angelou

On the second week of school, I (Marlena) was making the short commute to teach my first-grade class. As I waited at the stop sign, trying to picture all the fresh faces and remember their names, an ambulance sped by with sirens blaring. Going just out of sight around the bend in the road, the siren suddenly stopped.

I resisted the urge to turn left and drive by and instead continued to school. Later that morning, the principal notified me that Tommy, one of my students from the prior year's class, was in a car accident, and his outlook was not good. Immediately my mind replayed scenes from the previous school year.

Learning was serious business for Tommy. He couldn't ask enough questions or solve enough problems. Even in first grade, Tommy had a drive for curiosity that was rarely rivaled by his peers; in fact, his presence in class often made me wonder why so many children had already lost their natural sense of curiosity.

With a heavy heart, I attended the funeral for this child who was so full of life and creativity. I was completely unprepared for what I saw when I entered the church. One of the first assignments my students had completed in the previous year's class sat on an easel near the entryway. The assignment consisted of a photo of Tommy on the playground with his two best friends and a handwritten sentence. The inspiration for the assignment was a book titled *To Be a Kid* by Maya Ajmera and John D. Ivanko.

To Be a Kid is a book about kids from around the world doing what kids do best. The pages are filled with beautiful photographs of children enjoying friends, learning about the world, playing games, and being with family. Tommy's assignment was to use the sentence frame from the book, "To be a kid means…" and to finish the sentence.

Other students wrote statements like:

- To be a kid means to play soccer.

- To be a kid means to go to Disneyland.

- To be a kid means to have brothers and sisters.

In wiggly letters that Tommy had labored to make as straight as he possibly could—while yearning to run outside and hunt for butterflies—he completed the sentence.

"To be a kid means to never grow up."

I read it again, slowly.

"To be a kid means to *never grow up*."

At the time he handed his paper to me, I remember thinking to myself, *That's Tommy*. He was never going to grow up and lose the qualities that made him so special. He would always be a little mix of mischievousness, curiosity, creativity, and playfulness. Those same qualities also scared a few teachers, but it's what made Tommy so uniquely *Tommy*.

As I continued down the aisle to the front of the church, the next easel to catch my attention was Tommy's final project of first grade. After reading the story, *One Hundred Is a Family*, by Pam Muñoz Ryan, the students wrote a story about their family. As I remembered what Tommy wrote, a rush of emotions surged through my body.

Three Is a Family Going Camping, by Tommy. In the corner of his watercolor picture (Almost all the student-created art in my classroom was paired with a book and a written essay.), there was a tent with a dark shape inside.

When I asked Tommy to tell me about the shape in his picture, he said casually, "Oh, that's my baby sister."

"Tommy," I said, "*You don't have a sister.*"

"Oh," he informed me as his attention began to wander to something more interesting, "She isn't born yet."

Easels lined the aisle, containing almost every project that Tommy had completed in my class. I knew that everything these parents treasured from their son was displayed on the easels in this church. But I also noticed what was not on display.

Not one worksheet hung on the easels.

Not one photocopied worksheet.

Not one cut-and-paste project.

Not one color-in-the-lines paper.

These were all projects I had designed—projects that allowed Tommy to express his innermost self—and were what Mom and Dad cherished most. I was reminded that the moments of childhood are fleeting. We cannot measure how they will be treasured by families for many years to come, be it in their joy or their sorrow. Our students deserve to love every minute of their young lives and must be allowed to discover who they are within the safety of our classrooms.

As educators, our job is to help each student find their uniqueness. What I saw in Tommy's writing and artwork was that moments of exploration and discovery allowed us (me and his parents) to capture those precious moments—glimpses into Tommy's heart and soul.

Sadly, many children have already begun to lose their natural qualities of curiosity and creativity by first grade. And many teachers, out of fear of not being able to channel such energy, strive to keep kids in controlled environments. I've been guilty of this. But Tommy's short life often reminds me to value and foster curiosity, creativity, and playfulness in our students—and to develop those qualities into talents and skills for successful futures.

Creativity is as important in education as literacy.

—Ken Robinson

Marlena

Changing our mindset and being open to "possibilities yet unknown" is part of overcoming the "fear" of taking kids like Tommy into a deeper understanding of the world, and this is the challenge set before us.

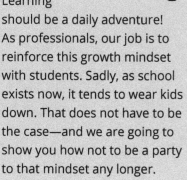

Jon

This is why we cannot let students equate worksheets with "learning" or "school." Learning should be a daily adventure! As professionals, our job is to reinforce this growth mindset with students. Sadly, as school exists now, it tends to wear kids down. That does not have to be the case—and we are going to show you how not to be a party to that mindset any longer.

Create a Formula to Suit the Problem

Julie was working on her senior college project, testing plane parts in the wind tunnel.

"You know," she slipped into our conversation one evening, "I don't follow formulas in math anymore. When I solve a problem, I have to create the formula to suit the problem."

"You make up the math formula?" I asked. "How do you know if you get it right?"

"Mom," she replied in her scholar-in-training voice, "there's more than one way to do it. I know what I want, I know the math; it's just a matter of adding in what I need to create the formula."

Really?

Can Mathematics Be Creative?

Maybe you know this; maybe *math people* know this, but I didn't. Not being especially fond of math myself, I never considered it to be a creative field. To me, math was something whose only purpose was to prove what was already known, to find the right answer. I once took a class called "Creativity in Childhood," and since then the developmental progression of creativity has intrigued me. I saw it in myself. I always saw it in children, but now I began to see creativity in new places: in math, science, history, and all sorts of disciplines.

How many times do we see the unknown as unworthwhile? Inspired by the creativity of a student, I learned to open my eyes and consider new possibilities—especially about areas I did not understand.

The question for all of us when it comes to our students is, *will we create new formulas to suit the problems?*

Chapter 2

Play by the Protocols

Simplicity is the keynote of all true elegance.

—Coco Chanel

So many trades have mastered the concept of protocols. But in education, we still lean towards two models: Use the overly scripted, corporately prepared lesson plan or bounce from freestanding lesson plan to lesson plan which offers no cohesion or flow to our students. A great coach, chef, or architect works within models and templates, but he or she also owns all their content—their signature dish or innovative approach to planning. (An excellent example of this is the *Chef's Table* series on Netflix. These professionals bring so much passion and creativity to one of our simplest daily pleasures: food.)

Does a chef have 365 daily breakfast recipes? No. That would be untenable. A chef might have a handful that they have truly mastered. People typically will say, "I bet a chef has less than a dozen remarkable breakfast dishes." How about a CrossFit trainer? Would they need a unique routine for every day of the year? Or do they have a core workout, with leg days, arm days, and some days where they work the entire body?

If you have played a sport, what would be the effect of not having a daily practice schedule? The answer is that game performance would suffer. Similarly, classrooms that do not have daily, weekly, and monthly protocols will, by the very nature of human learning, underperform compared to their potential. In practical terms, we define protocols this way:

Marlena

Think of it like this: You have a beautiful picture frame on the coffee table, but the print has faded some, and the kids have grown a little this past year, anyway. When the new prints arrive, you slip the old picture out of the frame and insert the new picture. Now you have a beautiful new picture on the coffee table again. EduProtocols, like the picture frame, stay the same. The lesson, like the print, easily changes, resulting in a whole new learning possibility!

You need to ship a wedding present to your nephew, and it just so happens the box is huge and heavy. You decide that the cheapest way to transport it is by train. You buy the ticket and send it on its way. Every day, that train makes the same trip at the same time, only the train carries different cargo each trip. EduProtocols, like the train carriage, stay the same. The content, like the cargo, changes for each trip.

EduProtocols:
The format stays consistent
while the content changes.

The Iron Chef EduProtocol emerged from the need to streamline delivery of content from teacher to student: share a slide deck, research, take notes, present in teams, score. (We detail this EduProtocol in Chapter 13.) The result was the same across the board: Kids could focus on the learning, collaboration, and creativity because they already *knew* the process. By teaching with EduProtocols, the *process* of daily work becomes nearly invisible, and the *content* becomes preeminent in the classroom. That's when massive growth occurs: when students are focused on the content.

Kindergarten student completes the Iron Chef EduProtocol using images.

Teaching with EduProtocols Makes Your Career Easier and Portable

Moved to sixth grade this year? Use the Iron Chef EduProtocol to teach Greek civilization. Another move to fifth grade next year? Use Iron Chef to teach the thirteen colonies. Master the math variation of Iron Chef while teaching fourth grade, and you are ready for any grade level using the same EduProtocol. If you are a high school teacher or move to the college level with five different classes this year, reduce your prep and use the same EduProtocols in all your classes, with different content for each course.

Do we teach for tasks or do we teach for content?

How many times has the method of teaching gotten in the way of your students learning? Instead of unintentionally making it more difficult for children to learn because we're actually teaching both the task and the content, let's develop EduProtocols: workflows which can be repeated with changing content.

Teachers often personally purchase lessons, and when the lesson is over, they buy another one. Every time the lesson changes, the brain load on kids (and teachers) raises their affective filter as they try to figure out what the task is asking them to do. Even in textbooks, we see dozens of graphic organizers, and since there are too many to memorize, each time the kids ask, "What do we do next?" or, "Is this right?" Teachers find themselves pushed to the front of the classroom answering questions about the mechanics of the lesson. The more kids focus on figuring out the task, the less brain power is available to understand the content, and the more they will rely on you for support.

Do we teach for tasks, or do we teach for content? If we teach for content, we can regain brain power by using EduProtocols to frame the changing content.

Marlena

This is why our cook has a defined repertoire of dishes. A cook cannot master a recipe if he is cooking up something brand new every single day of the year.

New Is Messy

As you read and reflect on your classroom, imagine EduProtocols replacing lessons. Think about how to teach the protocol until kids master the process and how you can use EduProtocols to deliver content all year long. Just like a chef, if you've mastered a few EduProtocols, you will have an infinite number of lessons at your disposal to educate anyone on any topic—with a minimum of preparation. The only materials you'll need to customize your EduProtocols are on the internet: Wikipedia (cite their sources), YouTube, and specialized websites have all the content you'll ever need for the raw materials included in your EduProtocols to cover any subject.

You might notice that as you begin to teach using the EduProtocols, students will struggle to understand what you are asking them to do. We expect this. It's new, and new is messy. Kids will have questions. They will make mistakes. So will you. You might not provide directions in the clearest manner. Your timing might be off. When it gets a little crazy, don't give up. Debrief with the class so they can learn the EduProtocol.

Ideally, use a particular EduProtocol for at least a full quarter. It takes about ten repetitions for students to become masters at the task.

EduProtocols can run once a week, once a day, or biweekly, but they should last all quarter, all semester, or all year. With practice, the needs of the protocol will move into the background, and the content will take the center front.

Then, and only then, can your students be free to enjoy the learning.

Marlena

A solid EduProtocol will become a trusted tool that makes content the focus for students, but it also stabilizes workflow for the teacher. Teaching is a big job; we need stabilization!

Marlena

Beginning with Smart Start activities as the preseason warm-up will help students ease into the EduProtocols with content later.

Marlena

Reps: the repeated practice, the repetition that we talked about earlier that we all need when learning something new. We over-focus on what kids are learning and forget to give students the time they need to internalize how to learn.

Our Eight-Point PROTOCOL Checklist

It is easy to confuse EduProtocols with other types of lessons and digital worksheets. EduProtocols are structured enough to be repeated, yet open ended enough that students can be creative and have choice in demonstrating their learning. The lesson design itself is fairly simple, with the goal of shifting the workload from the teacher to the student. What makes an EduProtocol? There are eight common characteristics of EduProtocols that make them powerful tools for teaching and learning:

1. **Protocol = Lesson:** If EduProtocol + EduProtocol + Edu-Protocol equals a unit, then one EduProtocol is somewhat equal to a lesson. They have substance and are not to be confused with "activities" which we might do within a lesson; for example, these are not protocols: quick write, pair share, gallery walk, exit tickets, elevator pitches, voting, sentence stems, writing what you learned in the form of a song, or folded-paper books for notes.

2. **Replicable:** An EduProtocol has a defined structure that can be repeated by other students and teachers. The Edu-Protocol should be named to provide it an identity and to separate it from the content.

3. **One to One:** Accountability for each and every student for a part of the activity is a key component of the EduProto-cols. The contribution is traceable and provides evidence of learning.

4. **Time Frame:** A fitness trainer wouldn't have a client do bench presses or squats for a full hour. Effective workouts have variety. EduProtocols should be ten to thirty-five minutes in length. Ideally, an EduProtocol does not use the entire class period, allowing students to work on multiple learning events in one period. Simplify the content so that it can be completed in the allotted time.

5. **Overtly Connected Standards:** An EduProtocol should feature multiple adopted standards (ten to twenty-five grade-level standards) in a single setting. Kids will strug-

> **Note:** *Do not confuse Smart Start singular-use activities, which are intended to build culture, with EduProtocols. Smart Starts might be protocols, but more likely they are activities with the specific purpose of getting the year off to a good start while building camaraderie and culture.*

gle on day one but will be rolling by day five. (See #1 and #2 under "Best Practices" below for reference.)

6. **Cs in Action: (Four Cs—Communication, Collaboration, Critical Thinking, and Creativity)** Do not turn your class into an Edu-gulag with unceasing fill-in-the-blanks-type work. Effective EduProtocols are not just worksheets. They embody open-ended learning and Universal Design for Learning (UDL) concepts. If your students don't like a protocol, you are likely doing it incorrectly.

7. **Open and Able to Be Used Across Multiple Subject Areas:** EduProtocols should work in multiple subject areas (an EduProtocol used for science would also be able to be used with social studies and language arts) or across multiple standards within a subject. (Math-specific Edu-Protocols could be used to teach the associative property as well as factor trees.)

8. **Loved by Kids:** Design for children! Take your teacher hat off and tap into your own innate creativity. Design something that's irresistible to students of many ages.

Best Practices with EduProtocols

Keep in mind the SPIRIT to which EduProtocols are designed as you deploy them with your students. Six tips to remember are as follows:

1. **Serious Commitment:** We always tell our own children, "If you are going to play a sport or be in a play, commit to the whole season." You can do the same by making the commitment to use the EduProtocol weekly, all semester, or all year long so students gain fluency with the process, which will enable them to focus on the content.

2. **Progression:** The EduProtocol begins quickly and easily. The first two reps of an EduProtocol should focus on a nonacademic, low cognitive-load task so students can concentrate on the task, not the content. Educators should simply focus on students completing the EduProtocols.

Quality may be low at first. Over time, add skills and subtasks or shorten the time frame to add intensity.

3. **Immediate Feedback:** If you are grading an EduProtocol any time other than immediately, your EduProtocol is in danger of losing student intensity. Athletes crave feedback. Chefs come out of the kitchen to see how guests enjoyed the meal. Develop for immediate feedback, and you'll find more immediate impact.

4. **Reps:** Jon's football coach, Mike Waufle, loved to say, "Reactions are what you do without thinking. The only way to get the very best results is to do a million reps." We can't do a million reps in class, but we can do twenty or thirty or more, and that's mastery learning.

5. **Interest:** Keep the pace just fast enough to hold the attention of kids with just the right amount of content for the right amount of time.

6. **Tech Balance:** Please use tools like Quizizz, Kahoot, Google Suite, Flipgrid, and others, but remember: Sometimes paper is faster. Brain research tells us a good old Frayer or Venn diagram on paper can be a super-efficient way to set up for the digital tools where ideas get synthesized.

How to Start?

Our desired state is that students, thoroughly familiar with the technology and the protocol process, can completely focus on the content. It is imperative to move into the EduProtocols with purpose and at a pace that is slow enough that all students can master the process first. We cannot stress this enough. Choose one EduProtocol, and when it's going smoothly, after using it weekly for about a month or two, start another. Work the EduProtocols into your curriculum slowly, one at a time. The students will adjust to this different way of learning, and you will adapt as well. Over the course of the year, your students should be able to master between

Jon

So I'm going to go back in my wayback machine to the year 2002. I'm minding my own business, teaching sixth grade, doing Latin roots. We get to the quarter-final test. Now, the quarter-final test is cumulative, right? And I want my kids to do well. So on Monday I give them the test, and my kids self-correct. Out of the forty-five words for the cumulative, we realized that many of us missed about the same fifteen. So I made those our words for the week. Guess what we did on Tuesday? We did the test. Guess what we did on Wednesday? We did the test again, with immediate feedback. I had about seventy-five kids, so when we got to Friday for the test, I didn't give anybody less than a B. I realized that I could massively increase their learning with this EduProtocol.

Don't raise your hand; I'm calling on everybody.

—Sam Patterson

four and seven EduProtocols. As Cori Orlando, K–6 tech coach, says, "Expect a learning curve, but don't give up."

The following year, as you have successfully built your capacity for teaching with EduProtocols, you will be able to introduce them more quickly to your students. Perhaps one or two per month until students build up a repertoire of EduProtocols to call upon. Refer to the list of Best Practices, but the most important one is this: Use the EduProtocols weekly!

Fast and Curious

Start your journey as follows: As soon as possible, Monday morning or perhaps tomorrow, try this entry-level vocabulary EduProtocol with an online quiz program such as Quizizz or Socrative to get you started.

In this EduProtocol we are going to use the quiz program for the instruction instead of for the test. The purpose of this EduProtocol is to teach vocabulary. This isn't necessarily the highest activity on the Four Cs scale, but we include it here because the greatest teaching benefit of this EduProtocol is recapturing the time spent introducing and teaching vocabulary—so you can invest in other EduProtocols.

There are a lot of great quiz programs out there: Kahoot, Quizizz, Socrative, Quizlet Live. But Quizizz is our favorite. Here's why:

Monday

It's Monday morning: vocabulary day for the new unit. When the kids come in, we immediately crank up the quiz. If we have fifteen words this week, let's say they get half of them right. (Notice it's not that they got half wrong; they got half right.) They now know what they know! Now, out of the fifteen, we've only got to focus on seven, and it's Monday. So take the words, and use the Quizizz feature where your questions turn into slides and hit Review Quiz. Click through the slides and give the kids immediate feedback. "The correct answer for this is this, and here's why, and there's the picture that goes with it." Repeat for each of the words.

Then do the test again, right away. Remember, reps build speed, and this is where we want speed. Do it twice on Monday. Quizizz gives you a class total on the fly. See how many kids have passed or not passed immediately. So imagine it's Monday morning, we've got fifteen new science words, we've got fifteen new math words, and we've got fifteen new spelling words. (What grade? Any grade, realistically.) The kids walk in, sit down, and do the test.

Based on how many they got right, give them a mini-lesson and run the quiz again. We can do this with *human children* in under fifteen minutes. Wondering what they're going to do for homework? They don't need homework. We're doing the work in class.

Thursday Is the New Friday

Tuesday morning rolls around, and it's the same EduProtocol. Give them the quiz again. The magic of this process is that what used to be two or three days a week of class time now takes much less time, and we gain those two days for other learning. We're not eliminating, we're automating. If we used to do the test on Friday, taking at least half of the class period, we just gave ourselves half of the class time back—every week for the rest of our career!

But let's say you want to get the kids more involved; you want them operating on a higher Four-C level. Once we do this EduProtocol for about three weeks, we outsource the test making. "Table four, you're making the test for next week." The students are now operating at a higher level because they must find the right pictures and carefully consider the information. This works all the way from fourth-grade kids working on state history to AP classes.

Why do we call it "Fast and Curious"?

First, this EduProtocols is a fast way to expose kids to words, which saves classroom time. Second, people are curious about their own abilities. *Reader's Digest* has tapped into that for decades with Word Power and quizzes such as, "How Artful Is Your

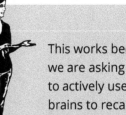

Marlena

This works because we are asking kids to actively use their brains to recall the words (with immediate feedback) instead of just looking up definitions or copying words from one part of a page to another. On day two, recall again. On day three, remember again. Bam! By the end of the week, the words have begun the move from short-term memory to long-term memory.

Vocabulary? Take our quiz to see if you've got a flair with artful words." Marlena's tenth-grade ELA teacher used Word Power in class every week to expose them to new vocabulary. It worked. The Encyclopedia Britannica has figured out that the more you take a quiz, the more you learn the words. As the *Encyclopedia Britannica* says, "The faster you answer, the higher your score. When you are done, try again to beat your best score."

As Jane McGonigal, American game designer and author, says, "We've been playing games since humanity had civilization—there is something primal about our desire and our ability to play games." People don't want to look up words; they want to play games, because it's human nature to be curious about our ability to know things.

Directions for the Fast and Curious Protocol

Prior to day one: Set up your quiz. (We prefer the question-to-flashcard and immediate class feedback features in Quizizz, but any quiz program will work.)

Day One

1. Quiz students. (Make sure students receive immediate feedback on their missed words.)
2. Review most-missed words.
3. Quiz again, ensuring immediate feedback.

Day Two

Repeat missed words from day one.

Day Three

Repeat missed words from day two.

Day Four

Conduct the final quiz or test.

Call to Action

This entry-level EduProtocol is an excellent way to experiment and see the impact protocols can have in your classroom. Use this activity tomorrow to kick-start EduProtocols in your classroom.

Note: *In the next section of the book we will discuss tips for developing class culture, which we have found to be beneficial in the successful implementation of EduProtocols.*

We further explain EduProtocols beginning with Chapter 15.

Chapter 3

Culture is Everything

Every child is an artist. The problem is how to remain an artist once he grows up.

—Pablo Picasso

Two students burst into my (Marlena's) sixth-grade classroom in an emotional tidal wave that only sixth-grade girls can channel.

"Mrs. Hebern, Mrs. Hebern!" they shouted as they slammed the door.

"Yes, what's up?"

"Rosa's aunt has cancer, and she just found out last night that she has one week to live. She's really upset. We want to play *The Fight Song* when she comes into class to show our support."

"Ok, that is an excellent idea. Let's do it!" (It is so easy to be on the good side of kids sometimes. This was a no-brainer!) Together we prepped the video to play when the kids walked into the classroom.

Everyone else was already in their seats in awkward sixth-grade excitement about the surprise, wondering what would happen next. Rosa entered the class and quickly realized the song was for her.

I put my arm around her shoulder, pulled her close, and whispered in her ear, "Your classmates care about you and wanted to play this for you. The whole class wants you to know that they support you."

When I let her go, her two best friends stood and gave her a hug. Within seconds, classmates began joining the class hug, slowly, at first, and then in a rush, until all students were in one giant embrace in the center of the room.

Jon

Why is culture so important? If we want the kind of classroom where students feel safe enough to try new things, we must first work purposefully to shape the culture before we ask kids to take risks.

Slowly, at first, and then in a rush.

In that very second, I stood back and realized that *culture was everything*. I had invested three months trying to build culture, patiently waiting to see the results of my efforts. And there it was.

Culture Is Everything

Most educators expect that the end-of-year field trip or big swim party will be the culminating event that brings kids to the emotional point of no return. When I was an eighth-grade student, my class wrote affirming notes to each other. I didn't have as many notes as some of my peers, but I was delightfully surprised to find that my classmates had nice things to say about me. Why wait until the end of eight years of school for such a powerful experience? Like many of my classmates, I could have used that experience years before.

How many times have you, as the teacher, felt your class gel together after the year-end event, only to see them move on to the next grade before the benefits of such bonding are optimized for learning? What's the solution?

Flip your class culture.

Real learning and creativity cannot take hold unless the classroom culture supports each and every student.

SMART START
EduProtocols

There are painters who transform the sun into a yellow spot,
but there are others who, with the help of their art and
their intelligence, transform a yellow spot into a sun.

—Pablo Picasso

It's the first day of school. (Cue the ominous music.)

One by one, the students enter the classroom. They look for friendly faces as they scan for open seats. A few sit in familiar clusters, laughing and sharing summer break stories. Others sit alone because they don't know anyone in this class. They glance nervously at the cliques and wonder if they'll ever be accepted or perhaps are thankful that they are not. It's hard to tell; the nervous smiles all look the same.

Mrs. Jones stands in the front of her class as the bell rings, a little unsure about how she will bring this class together.

First-Day Anticipation.

She greets her sixth-grade students as she begins to pace back and forth between tables two and five. She introduces herself and then launches into the most important thing she can think of for the first day.

"Let's go over the class rules," she says, as she walks to the side of the room and points to a poster. "The first one, follow all directions . . . ."

Fifteen minutes later . . . "Here is your school handbook." She passes a stack of materials to every table as each student silently takes one.

"Take your school handbook home and go over it with your parents. The signed slip is due back by Friday, or you will lose the ten points for this assignment."

The hour slowly passes.

Mrs. Jones glances behind her as she writes on the board with a squeaky black marker. A student in the back row tears off a corner of his notebook paper and places the tiny piece in his mouth. Mrs. Jones drones on, clearly enjoying herself. The student pulls apart his pen, and holding the tube in his right hand, places the wet wad of paper inside the makeshift blowgun.

"Wait! Hold on. Just *stop*!" We already know how this ends.

Mrs. Jones thoroughly enjoys teaching, knows her content, and loves kids. The routine is much the same every day: read, lecture, and answer the questions at the end of the lesson. Homework includes answering more questions and writing reports. Maybe a little project was thrown in occasionally so there can be a display for open house at the end of the year. The top third of the students will excel, the bottom third will struggle, and all the while, Mrs. Jones will have a terrific time lecturing and choral reading her way through the weighty textbook.

Though they're not sure why, the students are clearly not buying the status quo, and we shouldn't either!

Like camp! Yeah! Kids go to summer camp for four days, and then they are all CRYING that last day because they miss their new FRIENDS. Can't we do school like that? WE CAN!

Jon

Can't we start our class culture better than that?

There will be homework
that's never finished, learning never
realized, and a subculture of
resistance in this classroom.

Let's go back in time and repeat the first day of class, but with a Smart Start.

Smart Start Activity One

As soon as students take their seats, Mrs. Jones passes out playing cards to each student and tells them to find their matching card. Students find one another to form pairs.

"Say hello to your new friend. Today you are going to Frayer a friend." Mrs. Jones announces.

"This is a Frayer," she explains as she projects some quick samples on the board.

"In the center is your partner's name. You'll interview them and complete the four squares: Describe your classmate, four things they like, four things they do not like, and draw a picture of their dream pet. You have ten minutes. Ready? Go!"

The students get right to work.

Ten minutes later . . .

Frayer a Classmate

Describe your classmate. (What do they *look* like?)	What are four things that they *like*?
	1.
	2.
	3.
	4.

Name of Classmate

Draw a picture of their dream pet based on their description.	What are four things that they *do not* like?
	1.
	2.
	3.
	4.

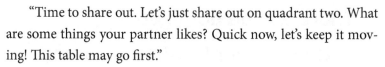

Jon

Only give kids ten minutes—less if you think they can handle it—since they will wait until the last ten minutes to do the activity anyway. Establishing a quick work cycle is critical for your class. Also, make sure kids complete all four facts. You are prepping them to provide multiple, defensible reasons for their answers.

Jon

Yup—look for groups, not silos. Listen, and when you hear, "I like _____" multiple times, you pounce on those.

"Time to share out. Let's just share out on quadrant two. What are some things your partner likes? Quick now, let's keep it moving! This table may go first."

A boy stands and begins to introduce his partner to the class. "This is Megan, and she likes pizza, Hot Tamales, and playing 40K—she has a team. And um . . . goofing around."

The class laughs,

"Thank you," Mrs. Jones says, "Megan, your turn."

Megan stands and begins to introduce her partner. "Alex likes cool bands, big hamburgers—well done—and he's the fullback on our football team."

"Next," Mrs. Jones urges as she points to a student seated at the table. "Your turn."

After fifteen minutes, the class has completed the first round. Mrs. Jones announces that the next round will be quadrant four.

"Now, I want you to find one person who has at least one thing that you both like in common. You've got two minutes. Stand up and go!"

The music plays, (upbeat, not ominous) and the students mingle. Mrs. Jones circulates the room, listening in to the groups which are starting to form. Once groups begin to form, she announces commonalities so that more students can find groups to join. Then she points to each cluster, and they announce their "thing."

"Now find another pair that shares another one of your favorite things." Mrs. Jones announces. As she hears students repeat a certain point of interest, she knows that other students probably share the same interest, so she announces that item to help students connect. Mrs. Jones wants students to find groups and discover their classmates are more alike than different.

The students once again mingle and partner up.

"Discuss *why* you like this and then find two other things that your entire group likes."

As they begin, the excitement in their voices rises.

"Let's share out." Mrs. Jones announces.

Each group quickly shares out their three commonalities.

"Now, quickly find other people who have a similar dream pet to yours." She waits as the class forms new groups. "Choose the best one in the group and be prepared to share it out." She circulates the room, leaning in so that she can hear the student discussions. She is gathering valuable intel and insights in real time about how her students interact with one another. "One minute to go!"

One by one, the groups share their chosen dream pet. Just before the bell rings, Mrs. Jones collects the papers for safe keeping.

Smart Start activity one, almost done. Mrs. Jones flips through the papers; however, she has a pretty good idea by now about who her students are and is getting to know them already.

The goal for the first day is for students to learn each other's names and find commonalities with one another, especially with students who did not previously associate with each other.

Now, on to Smart Start Activity Two; the day is *just* getting started!

Jon

This is Smart Start at its best. Knowing kids FAST. Lots of laughs ensue, and personalities are being revealed. You can create an end-of-the-year-level culture with only a couple days of activities like this.

Smart Start Activity Two

As the day progresses, Mrs. Jones will provide a mix of activities to help everyone get to know one another. They will play a name game and participate in fun games designed to build teamwork, such as Peter Skillman's "Spaghetti Challenge," in which teams build the tallest tower using a limited supply of marshmallows and dried spaghetti. They will read the *Huffington Post*'s "Cat Vs. Dog: War of The Diaries" and compare the lives of cats and dogs in a Venn diagram. They will share some laughs and learn that Mrs. Jones' class isn't going to be anything like last year's class. Everything's going to be different. And different is good.

This class is about student voice, working to support each other in a purposeful and meaningful way, and learning while having fun.

Over the next few days, Mrs. Jones will continue building upon the success of day one. She'll also use a jigsaw activity to help students become familiar with the handbook while getting students comfortable working with a new group of classmates. She'll

Jon

This is the chance to model: Novel ideas and creative thinking are premium in your class—many answers can be correct, but I swoon over divergent thinking. Let them get their freak flags out!

Marlena

And once class is up to full speed, students will need minimal help with the technology piece, freeing teacher and students to be immersed in the culture of the class and the learning experience without interruption.

Jon

We are teaching academics, but we're not enslaved to "standards." We are teaching kids how to think, how to process information, how to work together, and how good it feels to finish and receive feedback. Get students releasing dopamine all day long—they are ready to be addicted to your class.

keep mixing groups so that each student will have multiple opportunities to work with others. She will front-load her students' computer skills with boot-camp activities (scaffolded tech activities with a low cognitive load that focus on how to use technology over learning content) so they can become familiar with expectations for the year. Her goal is to break down established walls and stereotypes from prior years while front-loading students on the skills they will need to succeed in this class.

Smart Start is all about stealth learning.

Mrs. Jones will continue building on the foundation she started on day one. Introducing Smart Start activities, teaching tech boot camp, and then moving those activities slowly into the classroom using an introductory-level curriculum.

The Smart Start Story

Minarets High School was the first school-wide Smart Start program. And, like many groundbreaking inventions, the initial idea for incorporating Smart Start into the opening of the school was an accident!

I (Jon) realized, four days before the opening of a brand-new school, that if the kids simply strolled in, and teachers just started teaching (like we normally do), the school could never be truly different. If Minarets started the same as every other school, Minarets would end the same as every other school.

So I asked myself, *What are the essential things our kids need to be able to do by the end of the first week?*

There was an interesting juxtaposition here, because the staff had many experienced teachers for a new school, but they were inexperienced teaching in a classroom where each student had their own computer (also known as 1:1). The *eureka* idea was to provide teachers with guided lesson plans which would build necessary tech skills for students and teachers while building the culture of the school. Instead of wasting the first week of school where kids (pretend to) listen to the teacher recite the rules, there would be engaging activities.

The foundation of the Smart Start idea was to heavily en-culture the first week of the school year. It also created a chance for teachers to try new, fast-paced activities which were already scaffolded for them, like learning presentation skills through the Worst Preso Ever, using iMovie to share their movie heroes, or Frayering a Classmate.

The second half of the class period would be team building with the goal to destratify classes, helping kids get to know one another. On the first day of school, children walk into class and in-evitably sit by someone they know or someone in their peer group. Unless kids stretch beyond their social comfort zones, you're not extending their friend group, and everyone misses opportunities to learn. One of the *hidden agendas* of Smart Start was to *destratify the class* and get kids mixing and knowing the names, likes, and dislikes of kids with whom they would not normally talk—at that beginning of the school year "honeymoon" period.

Another goal was to extend the honeymoon period as long as possible so that instead of the first three weeks of school being cool, maybe the first six weeks or nine weeks of school could be. Sooner or later the early dynamics unravel a bit, but the longer the fresh engagement lasts, the longer students have to build trust with each other. This was the original DNA of the Smart Start idea. Cre-ate culture, scaffold better experiences for teachers leading kids, and purposefully destratify classes to avoid a segregated culture. And to this day, Minarets High School classes have remained rela-tively clique-free.

If these goals can be achieved schoolwide, they can certainly be successfully implemented in a single classroom.

Worst Preso Ever: An activity where students study and use presentation errors resulting in a deeper understanding of how to make great presentations.

Frayer a Classmate: An activity where students explore the use of the concept and vocabulary Frayer model to interview a classmate.

Smart Start is simply the process of holding off on the curriculum in order to build culture.

Marlena

Wait to dive into curriculum full steam until at least the second week. Fill the first week with low-tech or no-tech activities until all the students—or classrooms—have their devices. Students should dip into content with short, fun ventures into the curriculum and slowly scale up to full speed.

K–12 Smart Start Formula

The Start: Days 1–3

- Half of class = School-wide (or class-wide) team building
- Half of class = Teaching the handbook

For the first few days of class, split your class time between class-wide team building and learning the school rules and the student handbook. (Obviously, a school-wide implementation is ideal.) This includes a mix of fun and front-loading the knowledge every student needs to be successful, while learning the ropes for the particular school and classroom.

Dial Up: Days 4–5

- Half of class: "Tech Boot Camp" with quick activities to acquaint students with your preferred tech tools consisting of ten- to fifteen-minute bursts of mini-lessons
- Half of class: Soft start and previews of cool stuff that's coming

Spend half of the class time in tech boot camp where students are front-loaded with the technology skills needed for the year. Use the other half to take a sneak peek into curriculum for the year. Choose high-interest topics that will spike excitement and anticipation for the class.

Smart Start is your giant "hook" for the year.

The pacing of the class must find a balance: slow enough so kids understand, but fast enough to be fun. And fun is important, as these excursions into the curriculum will become your "hook" for the year. Take time to teach the EduProtocols students will need. Once instruction begins in earnest, the class will be able to avoid many common technology distractions, allowing content to remain in the forefront.

Approaching Speed: Days 6–9

- Scaffold into your regular schedule
- Transition into independent activities
- Add to your students' repertoire of new skills
- Settle into the routine

Know the routine that you want to establish with students, then begin to scaffold and transition tech boot camp. Select Smart Start activities with curriculum content toward the anticipated schedule. Select independent activities while continuing to add to the students' repertoire of new skills.

Into the Routine: Days 9–11

- Develop healthy habits for learning
- Continue team-building activities
- Keep practicing new tech skills

Students will settle into the routine for the classroom, which will continue through the year, but the work of building classroom culture does not stop. Classroom culture is not an eight-day process. Use the collaborative activities in this book to keep kids working with different subgroups in the classroom so they become increasingly comfortable working with each other. With structure and routine established, it will become easier to later break the rules in the interest of student agency.

Marlena

When needed, it is always easier to pull kids back in after initial routines are established rather than to establish routines later in the year because they are needed.

Marlena

It isn't that each activity will magically become the culture, the culture is the result of the shared experiences curated thus far.

Flipping the Class Culture

On your own, in your room, or in a school-wide setting, how do you bond a classroom of students together and build a culture? I (Marlena) asked myself this question as I faced a group of sixth graders for the first time. I decided to focus on a list of things that would impact kids the most, and before I knew it, a new culture had developed in my classroom.

Use these CULTURE tips to help you stay on track as you work with your students:

Create safety for kids to get to know one another.

Unite with one another through shared positive experiences.

Laugh and have fun.

Think about and encourage in-depth answers.

Up-tempo the pace to keep kids moving.

Remix activities to keep kids engaged in learning and with each other.

Establish structure for continued success into the school year.

The expectations we set and live up to every single day build the culture we want. If the shared experiences are positive, uplifting, and supportive, then these become the foundation of the class culture. Sadly, the same is true if they are negative, degrading, or frustrating.

And remember, Smart Starts are not intended for homework!

For the first two weeks, take advantage of every minute of class time for culture-building.

Jon's Story on the Importance of Names

In first grade, I (Jon) was in a combined first- and second-grade class in a Catholic school. A few months into the school year, we went on a field trip in cars because our school didn't have a bus. I wasn't one of the cool kids, so I got to ride in the car with a nun, one of the moms, and a few other uncool kids.

As you can tell, this wasn't traumatic at all. I didn't have many conversations with classmates, but when kids *did* talk to me, they called me "Short Stuff."

It didn't take long for one of the kids to yell, "Hey, Short Stuff!" This sparked the usual banter and frequent use of my nickname. Finally, the nun turned around in her seat and barked, "Hey you guys, call him by his name!"

One of the kids looked straight at her and defiantly declared, "We don't know *his name.*"

That was really hard to hear as a first grader. And it still stings to tell the story. But my point is, *what if we had had Smart Start at my school?* Other kids would have definitely known my name, and maybe they would have been friendlier to me after learning more about our similar likes and dislikes. As a result, perhaps the "Short Stuff" moniker wouldn't have materialized. They were judging me as a very quiet, short kid, but maybe they would have seen something else if we had gotten to know each other better from the beginning.

Guiding Principles of Smart Start

Culture is everything in a classroom. Well, almost everything.

Smart Start activities will set the stage for classroom culture. But their reach is much broader than culture alone. Smart Start activities provide a training ground for the EduProtocols which will follow. Through the Smart Start activities, we will guide our students into the *type* of learning they will be engaged in all year long: up-tempo, fun, and different. Their preseason Smart Start warm-up is just the beginning.

To get started, think about the essential things that you believe your students will need to be able to do by the end of the first and second week. Make a list and look for or create Smart Start activities to meet those goals while keeping these principles in mind.

Marlena

Learning classmates' names is the beginning of building classroom culture, where every child is valued and respected by everyone.

Marlena

And don't worry if more skills come up later that you didn't cover in the first two weeks. You are building the foundation now, but you will continue building upon that foundation all year long!

Smart START Guiding Principles

Smile: Keep it light, keep it fun, and maintain the fast-forward pace.

Teach: Instruct students to finish on time. One of the main principles of Smart Start is that the activity is almost always timed. At the end of the time, the teacher moves on to the next step. If students are talking and not finishing on time, that is your cue to shorten the time, not lengthen it. Students will learn to finish.

Activities: Activities should be designed to develop the culture along with tech skills so the focus can be on both content *and* creativity.

Routines: Routines will be developed through the cycle of the Smart Start activities. Keep them structured, yet fluid and flexible. The rest follows naturally.

Target Barriers: Everybody learns everybody's name. And find other commonalities among classmates to break down the barriers between student cliques and groups.

For the Teacher: Observe and learn the learning styles and needs of your students.

We've provided some of our favorite Smart Start activities in the following chapters. In addition, many team-building activities can be adapted for classroom use so all students can participate. Keep in mind the Smart Start Guiding Principles as you search for activities and plan your lessons.

Call to Action

Take a minute now to list the skills you want your students to have mastered by the end of the first week in your classroom or school (the essential things every student should know how to do to be successful). Save this list, as we will come back to it at the end of Chapter 12.

Chapter 5

Smart Start Tips for Littles

A person's a person, no matter how small.

— Horton, *Horton Hears a Who!*

Students as young as four or five can partici-pate in Smart Start activities as easily as old-er students. In addition to learning the names of peers, use concepts from each of the major units of study that will be ad-dressed throughout the year and create mini-lessons around each. These exercises will build success and confidence.

For example, students could learn to tell time to the hour with a partner. A simple task using a poem like, "When the big hand points straight up, and the little hand tells the time, it's three o'clock! Three o'clock! Bong, bong, bong!" Reinforce the poem with a clock-building activity. You have just successfully created a hook for the year by front-loading the expectation of telling time and helping students get to know a new partner. Every child will go home announcing that they now know how to tell time!

Repeat with other content in similar introductory-level activi-ties to ensure student success.

Marlena

Once you get to the unit on telling time, your students will have already mastered time to the hour!

Skills for the Year

Teach students how to log in to computers. Make "logging in" the lesson objective and provide username and password cards to scaffold the learning for as long as needed. When students can log in (in a reasonable amount of time), introduce mini "tech boot camp" activities. Keep building tech skills necessary for success: logging in, drag and drop, adding images, and writing in a text box.

Slowly move activities which use mastered skills into independent time. Other Smart Start activities may include cooperative games in PE to build teamwork and trust among students. Pair handbook rules with children's books that illustrate the concept behind the big idea. You can also use a hands-on activity or tech project to help students remember the main point.

Kindergartener practices logging in to an iPad.

The flow: Start with whole-class introduction of a Smart Start activity and then after about a week of replacing the Smart Start content with curriculum-embedded content, move into independent practice where students develop the capacity to choose from several activities and work on their own.

With classroom culture established through shared experiences, students will develop cooperation skills that last all year long and build confidence in their ability to master the curriculum.

Tech Boot Camp Tip: Logging In

When I (Marlena) was in high school, volleyball was a big deal. It seemed like everyone played before school and at lunch, just for fun. But one rule was strictly enforced: Before a player would be allowed on the court, he or she would have to bump the ball twenty times and then set the ball twenty times, without dropping it. This "tryout" policy kept the action on the court exciting, because all players had a minimum level of competency. It also minimized distractions due to excessive dropped balls and nonserious players.

Treat logging in for transitional pre-kindergarten, kindergarten, and first-grade students in the same way. Logging in is the entry-level keyboarding skill to the computer. Don't log in for the kids. Have your littles pass this basic, but essential, skill test before they can play on the court.

Adapting Smart Start Activities and EduProtocols for Littles

Most of the Smart Start Activities and the EduProtocols in this book are followed with a description of how to adapt the activity for the primary classroom. You will find tips and suggestions for successful implementation in your classroom.

Tip: *If logging in requires capital letters and the @ symbol, you will need to show students how to type these letters and symbols. Placing small colored dots on the keyboard and corresponding colored dots on their log-in cards can help students find the* shift, caps, spacebar, *and* return *keys.*

Call to Action

Create a list of the skills your littles need to know by the end of the first week and the first month of school. Look at your list for the natural progression of these skills. If you begin with logging in, list the remaining skills in the order of progression. As you plan Smart Start activities for your students, keep this progression in mind.

Chapter 6

Smart Start: Cat and Dog

I(Jon) first created this Smart Start activity for my high school English class, and it has since become a favorite across the grades. The silly diary of a cat and a dog—and the stark differences in their approaches to life—creates an upbeat opening activity for any classroom! Starting at 8 a.m. sharp, Dog's main focus is food, walks, and car rides. "8:00 a.m.: Dog food! My favorite thing!" Cat, on the other hand, is intellectual: "My captors continue to taunt me with bizarre little dangling objects. They dine lavishly on fresh meat, while the other inmates and I are fed hash or some sort of dry nuggets. Although I make my contempt for the rations perfectly clear, I nevertheless must eat something in order to keep up my strength."

Smart Start: Cat and Dog

Culture Goals

- Learn about your classmates.
- Practice working with peers.
- Practice sharing out in a class setting and listening to others.

Academic Goals

- Students learn how to use a Venn diagram.
- Students analyze text for meaning.
- Students practice coming to consensus in a group setting.

Teacher Big Ideas

- Make sure students understand the Venn diagram so you can use it throughout the year as an independent activity.
- Emphasize empathy for both the cat and the dog.
- Focus on groups coming to consensus before sharing out.

Description

Using the article, *JOKE: Cat Vs. Dog—War of The Diaries* by the *Huffington Post* (easy to find online) or a similar video of a cat and dog's diary entry from a first-person point of view, students will compare and contrast the journals in a variety of ways.

(Teaching note: Replace the "r-word" in the article with the term "brain-damaged" or remove the entire sentence.)

Prepare for the Activity

Step 1: Decide if the activity will be run from paper or from 1:1 computers or tablets.

Step 2: Make a digital version of the *Diary of Dog and the Diary of Cat* for the students or prepare to show a similar video.

Step 3: Photocopy a Venn diagram for each student like the one in Figure 1.

Step 4: Photocopy or prepare a digital version of the worksheet like the one in Figure 2 for students to complete individually.

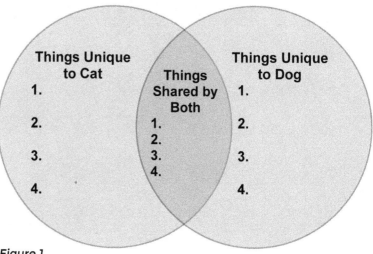

Cat and Dog

Things Unique to Cat
1.
2.
3.
4.

Things Shared by Both
1.
2.
3.
4.

Things Unique to Dog
1.
2.
3.
4.

Figure 1

Instructions

Activity 1: Read or watch the diaries together as a class.

Venn Diagram: Direct students to complete the Venn diagram for the Cat and Dog diary.

Activity 2: Cat and Dog Continuum

Have students indicate their preference of Cat and Dog by lining up on a continuum in the classroom or moving to the four corners of the room. On one side of the room are the total dog lovers, and on the other side are the total cat lovers. Choose students to discuss why they chose their particular spot on the continuum. Consider debating the merits of what makes each a "better" pet. Use sentence frames to elicit responses based on evidence. At the end of the debate, allow students to reposition themselves on the continuum and justify their new point of view.

Activity 3: Each student chooses either Cat or Dog and characterizes their choice using either a paper or electronic version of the handout shown.

Note: Up-tempo the activity (keep the pace moving) to set the pace for the year.

Frayer a Pet

Description	Your pet's name?	Action
What does your pet look like?		What does your pet do?
1.		1.
2.		2.
3.	Pick a name that reflects the personality of the pet in the example.	3.

Dialogue	What does the opposite pet think of your pet?	Interior Monologue
What does your pet say?	(In a quote)	What does your pet think?
		1.
		2.
		3.

Figure 2

Tip: Designate the person in the group who will be the speaker; for example, "Students wearing the most green will be the speaker in their group."

Activity 4: Students share in groups of Dogs and Cats. They report out to the class the best answer in each of the categories from their group. The purpose of this activity is for students to work together to come to a consensus and then to learn to use a sharing-out model where one student speaks for the group.

Activity 5: Let students choose one of four corners of the room (or the space between) with which they identify the most: likes cats, dislikes cats, likes dogs, dislikes dogs. Allow them to debate and "convince" others to change positions. If a student chooses to move, ask them to explain their reasoning.

Adapting for Littles

Activity 1: Using a class chart, each student will graph their favorite or dream pet.

Activity 2: Read aloud the same diary entries for Cat and Dog. (Tip: Remember to avoid the "r-word" in the diary.) As a class, graph the similarities and differences of Cat and Dog diaries on a large class Venn diagram chart.

Activity 3: With eyes closed, walk students through an imagery exercise about their pets. (Some children may not be comfortable closing their eyes. Allow them to sit quietly.) Ask, "How would you describe your pet? What does it do? What is its name?" Then ask children to draw a picture of their pet.

Activity 4: Help children find groups of students with similar pets. Share about their drawings from Activity 3 in the group. Come to a consensus about one funny thing or one interesting thing to share with the whole class. This may be difficult for younger students. Accept their efforts and remember that the goal of this activity is for them to discuss and agree on one thing to share.

Chapter 7

Smart Start: The Worst Preso EVER!

Jump-start presentation (or *preso*) skills in your students with The Worst Preso Ever Smart Start. In this fun Smart Start activity, students break all the rules of creating presentations while learning how to collaborate and develop quick presentation skills in the process. Once the rules are broken and understood, students will be ready to create presentations that are visually pleasing and organized. Of course, it still takes practice, so be ready to let your students jump right in! Jon created this activity after watching comedian Don McMillian's "Life after Death by PowerPoint" explanation about how not to make presentation slides.

Smart Start: The Worst Preso EVER!

Culture Goals

- Learn that time given for an activity will be limited.
- Learn to finish on time.
- Practice giving full attention to the task at hand.

Academic Goals

- Students learn basic presentation-building skills.
- Students practice the "soft skill" of speaking in front of the class.
- Students practice presenting.

Teacher Big Ideas

- Focus on finishing within the time limit.
- Students present someone else's presentation.

Marlena

It is imperative that students can justify a point, defend a position, or explain a process while speaking in front of a group: a key skill that students will need in college, career, and life.

Description

Delivering a presentation in front of the classroom two times a year is simply not enough reps for students to develop their presentation and speaking abilities. To counter the lack of structured practice for students, we have infused many of the Smart Start activities and EduProtocols in this book with presentation opportunities.

It takes many opportunities over the course of multiple years for students to become comfortable and deliver quality presentations in front of their peers. Making time for dozens of students to present can be a challenge, but build success by starting off with The Worst Preso Ever.

Prepare for the Activity

Step 1: Plan for 1:1 devices.

Step 2: Find on YouTube and bookmark the video "Life after Death by PowerPoint—Clean Edition" by Don McMillan or one of the many similar options.

Step 3: Make the basic template in the platform of your choice.

Step 4: Show students how to start building their slide deck.

Instructions

Activity 1

Step 1: Remembering to preview and make sure the video content is appropriate for your students, show students one of the following videos:

High School and Middle School: "Life After Death by PowerPoint" by Don McMillan

Primary: "Do's and Don'ts Worst Preso Ever: tinyurl.com/wpe-elem

Step 2: As you show the video, pause after each "no-no" and allow students time to take notes on what they should not do. The video covers such tips as too many bullet points, too much data on a slide, and animation vs. effectiveness.

Step 3: Each student builds one slide per rule broken and labels each error.

Step 4: Fun twist at the end: Students present a peer's slide deck, not their own. This really makes it fun and impersonal, allowing the kids to be emotionally detached from the slides.

Marlena

Yippee! This is evidence that the culture we are trying to instill in our students is starting to take hold.

Summary of the Build Process for Students

Choose a Topic	Break one rule per slide	Five Per Deck	Connect
Students choose a topic that they like or dislike. Pets, sports, food, bands, etc.	The goal is to highlight the errors; too many broken rules on a slide creates a jumbled mess!	Break a total of five rules per student deck.	List the rule being broken on the slide.

Tips: Don't teach the whole class all at once or from the front of the room. Circulate the classroom and help, depending on the needs of small clusters of students. We find that in large-group instruction, a third of the students already know the skill and are insulted that the teacher is wasting their time, a third might need help and might need another rep to really get it, and a third won't understand your directions no matter what you do and need one-on-one help. Students will eventually end up helping each other if you allow them to work in collaborative groups.

Presenting the slides

Presentation	Student Feedback	Secret Plot Twist
Each student presents a classmate's slide to the whole class in a timed two- to three-minute block. Expect kids to get in front of the room and to have a fun time.	Choose three to five students to sit in front of the room to give feedback to the presenters using an electronic format or paper and pencil. (Think *American Idol*.) Feel free to dish out titles: Paula, Simon, Randy, Ellen. The goal is to make it fun but also to move the voice to the students. The teacher, "Ryan Seacrest," moves about the room as the moderator, supporting the presenter, correcting errors, explaining processes.	Don't tell students ahead of time, but they will be presenting someone else's slide deck. This exchange adds a layer of fun to the activity, but in the moment of chaos, the students begin to understand and embrace the wrongness so that they can appreciate the rightness.

Tip: Establish tempo and keep the presentations moving along. Embrace the Four Cs (Creativity, Critical Thinking, Communication, and Collaboration), and let your class enjoy the fun that's guaranteed to follow.

Expect that a few students will go over the top with creativity or tech techniques, which may impress the other students. They will begin to ask, "How did you do that?" Allow them to learn from one another. This is budding collaboration.

Key Points to Remember

- Students will present someone else's presentation. It is important they are not presenting their own slide deck so that no one will have their feelings hurt, and everyone walks away a winner.

- After the presentations, pull in some higher-level critical-thinking skills by having students write a blog, top three skills essay, or slide deck on what they learned about creating presentations.
- Keep the activity fun and moving along so students stay engaged and interested. Help students understand that you're looking for effort, and that they need to focus for the entire time allotted. Teach them to finish.
- Pacing during presentations is crucial for this activity. Keep it moving. And remember, these first presentations will likely be awful, but over time they will improve.

Adapting for Littles

When creating a presentation, it would be simpler to tell students to add one picture and one word per slide, but they would not understand why this was important. Use this format to help students identify and create stronger presentations. After you watch the YouTube video, "Life after Death by PowerPoint" by Don McMillan, translate the information to the students in small bites. Be sure to use the clean version of the video. (One version uses the word *hell*.) Or choose an alternate video and play it one mistake at a time.

Focus on one simplified skill at a time, such as "too many pictures on a slide." Ask students to make two slides, one really good one and one really bad one. The good one should have just one picture, and the bad one can have lots of pictures. Remember to have students reiterate the difference between the good slide and the bad slide during the presentations. You might consider pre-formatting the slide deck with the titles "good" and "bad."

Students in the primary grades will need more time and direct instruction for adding images and formatting text, especially if this is their first time using a slide program. In subsequent projects, work toward a shorter work time to keep students engaged and on task.

Presentation Mistakes for Littles:

1. *Writing everything you will say*
2. *Long list of bullet points*
3. *Words everywhere!*
4. *Too many pictures*
5. *Misspelled words*
6. *Bad color combinations*
7. *Excess animation*
8. *Too many fonts*

Variation 1: Pechaflickr

Search Pechaflickr with a keyword, and Pechaflickr will randomly generate a series of self-advancing slides based on the term (subject) entered. Enter "farming," and several random images of farming and farmers will appear.

This makes for a fun activity when the teacher chooses the topics, and then students take turns presenting each slide. As students learn to speak extemporaneously in a presentation based on images, they hone their ability to synthesize information quickly and become agile presenters.

Variation 2: PechaKucha

A traditional PechaKucha presentation contains twenty slides that automatically advance after twenty seconds. These popular presentations are sometimes known as Japan's version of TED Talks.

For the classroom, twenty slides is likely too many. Choose the number you feel is appropriate for your students. Also determine the topic and the duration for each automatically advancing slide; for example, students will create five slides that advance every ten seconds. First attempts will be more successful if students develop the presentation around an interest or self-reflection on their goals or the growth they have seen in themselves before moving to academic content. PechaKucha presentations are carefully planned and rehearsed. They work well in the classroom setting because the presentation time is clearly defined.

Variation 3: PowerPoint Karaoke

In teams of six, students research and create their own presentation, then present a presentation created by another group without seeing the slides in advance. (Each student presents one slide.) Students will learn that knowing the topic is a huge advantage! Advance the slides automatically, as in the PechaKucha activity above.

Chapter 8

Smart Start: Frayer a Classmate

Students learn to use the Frayer Model by interviewing and **Frayering a classmate.** The Frayer Model was created by Dorothy Frayer in 1969 as a way for students to learn analysis of concepts. The traditional Frayer has four fields in which students provide a definition, characteristics, examples, and non-examples of a word or concept to deepen their understanding of word meanings. Due to the format and structure of the Frayer Model, it not only works for vocabulary but also for math, science, and other concepts. Students are encouraged to use images in the example and non-example fields.

Smart Start: Frayer a Classmate

Culture Goals

- Help kids learn the name of their classmates.
- Get kids to become familiar with their classmate's likes and dislikes.
- Practice communication skills.

Academic Goals

- Students learn the Frayer Model for vocabulary and note-taking.
- Students practice providing multiple correct answers.
- Students are challenged to provide deeper answers.

Teacher Big Ideas

- Emphasize having four facts for each category.
- Art does not count as much as ideas.
- Focus on moving around the room.
- Teach students to speak at appropriate volume levels.
- Give students specific time limits for each activity and teach them to finish.

Description

Students get to know their peers by finding similar likes and dislikes between classmates while learning a valuable tool for concept and vocabulary development.

Frayer Examples

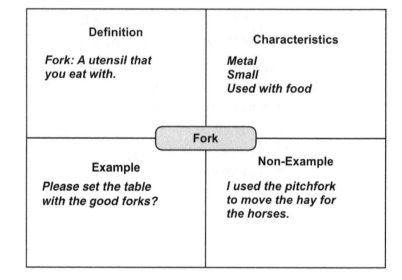

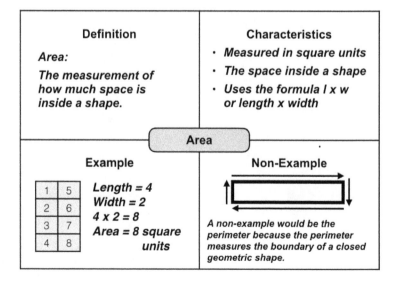

The Frayer also makes for a great hack for Smart Start activities and other topics throughout the year. We use it here, as a Smart Start activity, to Frayer a Friend.

Describe your classmate. **(What do they _look_ like?)**	**What are four things** **that they _like_?** 1. 2. 3. 4.
Name of Classmate	
Draw a picture of their **dream pet based on** **their description.**	**What are four things that they** **_do not_ like?** 1. 2. 3. 4.

Prepare for the Activity

Copy the Frayer a Friend activity for students, provide an electronic version (drawing programs work well), or fold paper into four squares and allow students to label their own.

Instructions

Step 1: Explain what a Frayer is by showing model examples readily available online. Search images of Frayer examples.

Step 2: Have students fill out a Frayer on a classmate—having four facts per category is critical.

Step 3: Share out.

Step 4: Ideas for connecting:
- Have students form groups based on likes using common themes used in typical student Frayers such as sports, music genres, or after-school favorite activities. Designate spots in the room for the groups to meet up and share. Change the topics after students discuss for a few minutes.

- Have kids re-form groups based on typical student dislikes, such as food or pet peeves.

- Have students vote and come to a consensus on a favorite picture from each cluster and share out.

Variations

1. In groups of four, create a collaborative dream pet from the best qualities of each participant's pet in the group. Draw or use construction paper scraps to create the new pet.

2. Use the Frayer on day six or seven to record memories of the first week of school. Consider asking students about their favorite memory, least favorite memory, and the characteristics of the class as a whole.

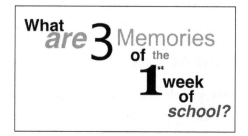

Key Points to Remember

- Allow students to find commonalities with other students in more than one way. This helps students discover they are interconnected with their classmates.

- Use the Frayer all year long. It's a versatile tool.

Adapting for Littles

- Walk students through the Frayer fields. Younger students can draw instead of write. Consider shortening to two fields instead of four or filling in one box a day over the course of four days. (Developing a Frayer over time is a great way to make a concept stick.)

- Introduce the Frayer using paper (because your littles are likely still trying to learn to log in to the computer) and then move the Frayer into an electronic drawing program in a few weeks. They will know just what to do with it when they see it on the computer.
- When they are working on the computer, provide images they can drag and drop into their drawing or word cards with searchable words.
- Give students an opportunity to share out with their peers about the person they interviewed. Facilitate students to meet up in groups by likes and dislikes.

Chapter 9

Smart Start: Things That Rock

The idea for Things That Rock came to me (Marlena) one day when I was preparing to teach sixth grade after being out of the classroom for five years. I hadn't chosen this teaching assignment, and had mixed feelings about taking it on. I'd never fully taught sixth grade before, but I wasn't too worried. *After all, school didn't start for another three months.*

Wrong. Class was to start that very day!

It was only the second of June! How could that be?

It was right there in the staff meeting notes from the day before. *I knew I should have attended that staff meeting!* The students were gathering for an overview of the next grade level and an activity we called "Flash Forward." All forty-four graduating fifth graders would be coming my way.

"No problem," I reassured the principal, "I got this!"

In reality, I had no idea what we would do. My mind was a blank. Well, not totally blank. I had tons of cool activities up my sleeve, but nothing seemed right for keeping a group of fifth graders engaged for thirty minutes—without technology.

It took me all of three seconds to realize I needed to channel my good friend, Obi-Wan Corippo, and the answer would magically appear. I closed my eyes in anticipation, and of course, inspiration struck like a lightning bolt.

Things that suck!

Jon

How about the title, "Things That Are Not Optimal."

HAHA!

Marlena

Really? These are sixth graders. How about *Things That Are Stupid*?

You can't win them all, Corippo.

"Things That Suck" is a well-known Edcamp session created by Dan Callahan, carried on by Bill Selak, and reproduced by Jon Corippo and dozens of others across America. A slide with a topic such as "ungraded papers" is shown on the big screen. Teachers place themselves along a continuum to indicate like or dislike for the topic. Then the discussion begins as they explain their points of view.

As I knocked out thirty slides in ten minutes, I realized the name of the activity wasn't appropriate. I headed to my personal learning network, otherwise known as friends on Twitter, for suggestions.

Finally, taking Mark Hall's suggestion from Edcamp Yosemite, I called it "Things That Rock."

I realized I wasn't just visiting these kids for a half hour; in mere months these kids were going to be mine for a full 180 days. This was going to take a lot more than being cool for five minutes.

As the slides came up on the projector, students moved about the room, chose their side, and declared their preferences on topics such as homework, lunchtime, and missing the bus. Then, calling on two or three students at a time, they discussed their choices.

The kids had fun, and the activity was as engaging for them as it was for the Edcampers.

As a teacher, I found this activity to be incredibly insightful into my students' thinking. I was surprised, for example, to hear that they did not like having 1:1 Chromebooks in the classroom, although, as the year progressed, I discovered this was because former teachers mainly used computers for writing and packaged practice programs that were not grounded in the Four Cs.

Smart Start: Things That Rock

Description

As students place themselves along a like/dislike continuum regarding a particular topic, such as homework, students will learn about the likes and dislikes of classmates and the reasons behind those feelings. Teachers will gain valuable insight into the makeup of their class as students discuss their opinions.

Prepare for the Activity

Create a slide deck of five to twenty with images or words to represent the topics of high interest to the age group of your students.

Consider the following prompts:

- Homework
- iPads
- Dodgeball
- Friend drama
- Ungraded papers
- Friends
- Teachers
- Rules
- Bullies
- School projects
- Lunchtime
- Tech that doesn't work
- Missing assignments
- Missing the bus
- People who yell
- Math
- Project partners who don't do their share of the work
- Backpacks

Culture Goals

- Students learn that their opinion matters.
- Get kids familiar with their classmates' likes and dislikes.
- Students learn to listen to and respect the views of their classmates.

Academic Goals

- Students practice providing multiple correct answers.
- Students are challenged to provide deeper answers.
- Students learn to base answers on evidence: in this case, their own feelings.

Teacher Big Ideas

- Use this activity to get to know your class.
- Practice attention-getting signals.
- Keep it fun by keeping it fast: about twenty items in thirty minutes with a quick pace.
- Allow students to respond to one another as long as they are good sports.

- Working alone
- Chromebooks
- Writing
- Detention
- Little brothers and sisters
- Seeing the principal
- Reading a book
- Recess

Instructions

Step 1: This can be a rowdy session depending on your class, so be sure to set up a norm to quiet students and recapture their attention.

Step 2: Indicate one side of the room as being "lame" and one side as "rocks."

Step 3: Explain to the students that they will physically move to the sides of the room to indicate their preference.

Step 4: Call on two to five students to give their reasons for choosing the way they did in the form of a quick statement. Avoid long dissertations, as other students will quickly become bored.

Step 5: Move to the next topic and repeat!

Step 6: Keep the pace moving so kids won't get restless.

Key Points to Remember

- We can't emphasize this enough: Keep the pace fast. Teach and use signals to bring student attention back to you so the activity can move forward.
- Be aware—at all times—of opportunities to develop a positive culture in your classroom.
- After the activity, when you have a few minutes of quiet, take note of your impressions and insights into your students.

Adapting for Littles

- This activity is appropriate for students of all ages. For younger students, be prepared to help them understand the concept of standing on a continuum based on their preferences. Start with something very concrete for the students, such as "peanut butter and jelly sandwiches" or an especially divisive topic, such as "eating peas."

- The greatest challenge will be helping young students understand that their vote counts for them and to not just go along with the crowd. Cori Orlando, tech coach extraordinaire, has her students close their eyes and point to a desired location prior to moving to establish choice to minimize the influence of peer pressure.

- Teach them to raise their hands to share *why* they made the choice. Cori also uses sentence stems such as, "I chose ___ because ___" to help littles coherently frame their thoughts. Be patient with rambling stories while directing; that's just what littles do.

Chapter 10

Smart Start: Paper Airplanes

Who does not like to fold a paper airplane and test the limits of flight? Add the element of challenge, and you have the makings of an engaging Smart Start activity. The idea for this Smart Start activity came about when my (Marlena's) daughter, a young engineering student, planned a visit to my classroom. I wanted her to teach a design activity, and we planned a modification of this one together. It turned out to be a fun team-building activity that fit well in the Smart Start model.

Smart Start: Paper Airplanes

Culture Goals

- Students learn to work in teams.
- Students listen to each other.
- Students work to solve a problem.

Academic Goals

- Become familiar with processes you will use in design or science projects.
- Students explore how the first answer, or first plan, is not always the best.

Teacher Big Ideas

- Develop routines. (Think about how you want to establish routines, like distributing and collecting materials, which can also be implemented in science class or other projects. This is the perfect time to teach those habits.)
- Scale it up or down depending on the age of students.
- For success, keep the math at review level (or don't include at all).
- Keep it simple. (If all you do is design airplanes and redesign airplanes in teams, that's enough.)

Description

In teams, students create paper airplanes and test them for flight distance and air time, then modify the airplanes for improvement.

Prepare for the Activity

Step 1: Find a space outside. (Airplanes may be flown in the classroom for younger students.)

Step 2: Get enough tape measures for students, ideally one per group. (Rulers or yardsticks may be more efficient for younger students.)

Step 3: Find some chalk or playground game cones. (Cones can also be used to mark off the flying field to make measuring easier.)

Step 4: Mark a starting line with chalk and mark ten-foot intervals with playground cones or a chalk line on the flying field.

Step 5: Allow one person from each team a few trial runs, and then on a "Ready, set, launch!" signal, students launch their airplanes all at once.

Instructions

Step 1: Provide paper, scissors, scotch tape, and a few paper clips for weights for each group. (Paperclips are useful for weighting the nose of the airplanes for longer, straighter flight.)

Step 2: Allow fifteen minutes for students to design as many paper airplanes as they wish in groups of two to four. Teams must come to a consensus on one design to test. (Make sure students write a team name on their airplanes.)

Step 3: Allow fifteen minutes for the class to test and note the length of flights using the chalk lines previously marked on the playground.

Step 4: Measure. Students will use these marker lines to determine the distance traveled.

Step 5: Redesign (ten minutes) and retest.

Step 6: Debrief the process of iterations and working in teams: worked, didn't work, and how to improve.

Marlena

This design-thinking process is important to help students realize that the first time isn't always the best version, be it airplanes, writing, or solving math problems! Iterations improve outcomes.

Variations

Explain the forces on the airplane: drag, thrust, lift, and weight.

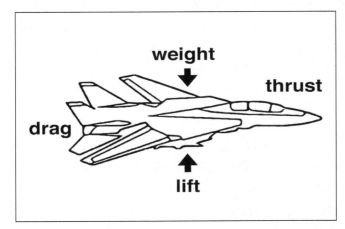

Ask students to keep these forces in mind during their build and flight time. (The purpose is to familiarize students with the technical terms and to get them thinking about why airplanes can stay in the air.)

Time

Allow students to time the flights using a stopwatch.

Graph

Depending on the grade level, figure the area of the wingspan using the length of the airplane and the width of the wingspan. Record flight distance in relation to the area of the wingspan. Graph the data as a class. Debrief the data, looking for trends in the design and times. For students who have not learned area yet, try tracing the outline of the wings on graph paper and counting the squares to discover the area.)

Variations

Trisha Sanchez, a seventh- and eighth-grade teachers explains how she uses the paper airplane Smart Start:

The activities help students become more open minded, not constantly judging the ideas of themselves or others, thus opening them up to be able to ideate more quickly and abundantly. Additionally, students begin to understand that following rules too strictly, thinking there is only one solution, and being fearful of taking risks holds them back from being creative. In the second week, students begin to move past those creative blocks.

Description

Teams will have eight minutes to make as many paper airplanes as they can. The team with the most planes over the finish line wins.

There are two rules:

- Three minutes to strategize
- Five minutes to build

After the contest, Trisha likes to ask the kids if they broke any of the paper airplane "rules" and why.

Trisha uses this Smart Start at the end of the school year to jump-start the next year. She created a two-week intro to focus on aspects of the design-thinking process as well as to help students be more creative and generate more ideas. (Trisha has her students for two years. Marlena's school also used Smart Start at the end of the year in the flash-forward activity where all students moved to the next year's teacher for an introductory period.)

Doing Smart Start at the end of the year keeps students engaged when they would otherwise be "checking out." It also gives them a glimpse as to how we will work next year. My hope with this unit is that my students see they can be creative, learn to design, and have innovative ideas.

Key Points to Remember

- Data gathering is a skill you will want your students to use all year long. Think how you want to have students do this and establish those routines here.
- Working in teams and coming to consensus are important skills. Help teams that are struggling to find common ground. Remind them that they will be able to redesign midway through, which will allow them to use another design if they wish.

Students test their paper airplanes in the classroom and measure the distance flown.

Adapting for Littles

- Use teams of two instead of groups of four.
- Allow for lots of test flights in the classroom as they try to make a paper airplane that will fly. Designate one end of the classroom (perhaps the "carpet area") for this. Don't be tempted to have the entire class make one style of airplane, but allow time to show and help small groups of students if they do not know where to begin. If one student has a successful flight, even if short, stop the class and ask that student what made his airplane fly. Provide tips and clues to the other students without falling into a "mass produced" scenario. If young students want to help other groups, let them. This is part of the culture we want to instill though the Smart Start activities.
- Expect distances to be *much* shorter, and the final flight may be able to take place indoors.
- On data collection, focus on distance traveled. Allow students to use rulers or yardsticks to measure.

- Record data in one large class chart. (Debrief the chart the following day. Don't extend this activity any longer or students will become too restless.)
- Allow time for students to work with peers and design many iterations. Let students vocalize their thoughts on why their airplanes performed the way they did without getting too technical. Sentence stems may be useful to help littles frame their thoughts, "One thing we did was_____. One thing my team needs to work on is _____." Remember, keep it light and fun. Step in as needed to prevent frustration.

Chapter 11

Smart Start: Cardboard Challenge

Filmmaker Nirvan Mullick discovered nine-year-old Caine Monroy's cardboard arcade in 2012. His short film about Caine's Arcade, built of cardboard in his dad's auto parts store, went viral. It inspired the Global Cardboard Challenge, in which children design and build cardboard arcade games from recycled materials. Caine's Arcade makes for an epic Smart Start activity. But this isn't a small-scale project and would be best tackled in mid- or late-September or October. The Cardboard Challenge can be used as a powerful culture-building activity if planned and timed correctly.

Smart Start: Cardboard Challenge

Culture Goals

- Students learn how to work with peers toward a common goal.
- Kids bond while having fun and solving problems.
- Students learn to listen to and respect their classmates.

Academic Goals

- Prepare and present in front of their peers.
- Practice problem-solving skills.
- Find more than one solution for solving problems and designing.

Teacher Big Ideas

- Concentrate the mess into fewer days by clearing two full days of build time.
- Incorporate writing and presenting into the structure of the activity.
- Expect a big mess.
- Use the camaraderie that comes from doing the unusual to extend culture building.

Description

Students create arcade games using cardboard, tape, and paint.

Cardboard arcade game is ready for play.

Prepare for the Activity

Step 1: Collect a variety of cardboard boxes in different shapes and sizes. At least one box per team of four students plus some extra pieces. Remember, if you bring in huge boxes, students will use them, so be prepared to handle the projects they make. You will also need the following:

- One roll of clear packing tape per every two projects
- Scissors for cutting cardboard
- Paint or markers

Step 2: Decide what basic supplies you will provide and whether you will allow students to bring additional supplies such as marbles, balls, and prizes.

Step 3: Prizes: Students may bring old fast-food toys they no longer use as prizes or other recycled items. Consider issuing tickets as prizes that participants can trade for popsicles or bags of popcorn, but remember that prizes are optional for a great Cardboard Arcade.

Key Points to Remember

- Take time to reflect. Allow students to learn from the activity. Student insights such as, "I've learned that teamwork is essential in ____" or, "I still don't like teamwork very much because____ " or, "I also learned things don't always come out as planned____" are valuable growth points for learning.

- Following the arcade, students write and present a two-minute TED-style talk on their experience.

- Consider providing necessary materials, but allow students to embellish from home.

- Students tend to overpromise and underdeliver, so the rubric (figure 3) was designed to help students be realistic about what they could provide. The teacher has the final say on all projects, but you will find that very few will need adjustments if expectations are clear ahead of time. (For example, darts are probably not a good idea!)

- Allow about three days for building. Consider concentrating the mess into two full days rather than building for forty-five minutes per day over three weeks.

- Invite younger students to the arcade to play the games managed by the older students.

- Plan a night for parents to visit the arcade. Or create a class video to share.

Inspecting goggles that will be used as part of a cardboard arcade game.

Variation

Mini 20% Time Project

Since this Smart Start project will ideally take place in late September or October, it is practical to further extend it into the curriculum. In preparation for implementing 20% Time Projects later in the year, consider using the Cardboard Challenge as a mini-unit to introduce the format students will then use. Students design their project and present their idea in front of the class as a team, which is scored according to the rubrics shown in figure 4.

Formal Project Oral Proposal Rubric
Caine's Arcade Cardboard Challenge (Figure 3)

Criteria	Needs Help. Proposal Needs Revision. 1	Project Is Almost Ready. Proposal Needs Revision. 2	Project Is Planned and Ready for Building! 3	Points
Summary of game, how it is played	Summary is not easily understood or needs much more information.	Summary is clear but needs more information.	Summary is clear.	
Structure of prizes (tickets, toys, etc.) and "value: of the prizes	Structure of prizes is not thought out and organized or is too complicated.	Structure of prizes is clear but slightly incomplete.	Structure of prizes is clear and easily understood and explained.	
Audience	Game is not appropriate for target audience. (PreK–2nd)	Game is appropriate for target audience.	Game is appropriate and compelling for target audience.	
Materials that you have and can donate	List isn't included.	List partially included.	List is included in full.	
Materials that you will need to purchase and cost (include who is purchasing these)	List isn't included or isn't practical.	List is partially included.	List is complete.	
Diagram of the game. Include approximate size. If the game has moving parts, include how those will work.	Diagram is not included or is not understandable.	Diagram only partially understandable and/or not complete.	Diagram is clear and readable.	

Formal Project Oral Presentation Rubric
Caine's Arcade Cardboard Challenge (Figure 4)

Criteria	Keep Practicing!	On Your Way!	Doing Great!
Oral Presentation: Delivery	Minimal eye contact with audience. Mostly reads from notes. Speaks in uneven volume with little inflection.	Direct eye contact with audience, but still relies heavily on notes. Speaks with volume and inflection.	Holds audience attention. Speaking is interesting and shows passion.
Oral Presentation: Organization	Is unfamiliar with the information. Does not adequately support the subject. Includes minimal data or evidence.	Presentation flows easily. Has a somewhat clear purpose but does not adequately elaborate. Some examples.	Presentation flows easily. Has clear purpose and adequately elaborates. Provides examples to support main idea.
Oral Presentation: Posture	Slouchy posture/ distracting gestures (leaning on something, side turned to audience, etc.).	Good posture, keeps focus, distracting gestures are minimal.	Shows good posture, keeps focus.
Oral Presentation: Language	Excessive use of "uh," "er," "yeah," "ya know," "like," etc.	Some use of "uh," "er," "yeah," "ya know," "like," etc.	Minimal use of "uh," "er," "yeah," "ya know," "like," etc.

Adapting for Littles

- Your younger students can participate in the Caine's Cardboard Challenge as well! Consider working with a "buddy class" to create the arcade games. Provide guidelines for the older students to ensure they are helping and not taking over the design-and-build process. Or have your littles work with a partner instead of groups of four.

- Making a board game is a fun alternative to building arcade games. However, we encourage you to try Caine's Cardboard Challenge. Littles have wonderful imaginations, and bringing their ideas to fruition is an empowering experience for them. Try lighter cardboard such as shoe boxes instead of thick cardboard so littles can cut it by themselves.

Chapter 12

Culture: It's Never Too Late

Whoever controls the media—the images—controls the culture.

—Allen Ginsberg

Building culture doesn't end in the second week of school. Now that you have carefully built up a positive class culture, and students are beginning to connect and show empathy for one another, shift your attention to *maintaining* the culture. All year long, dip into new Smart Start activities at least once a month throughout the year to help students reconnect.

Positive class culture shows up when you least expect it.

Just as I (Marlena) found with my sixth graders, class culture takes time to build, and the evidence is not always obvious to adults. But the effort will have lasting effects on kids.

Where to Find More

With your new understanding of Smart Start activities and the intended purpose of culture building, you will able to find more activities for your students that meet the goals you have defined for the end of week one.

Search for party games, icebreakers, or team-building activities that can be modified and adapted to the classroom. Consider how you might change these with a writing component to build an academic connection. Also consider school initiatives, such as cyber-safety or bullying, and how you might create Smart Start activities around those themes to reinforce the desired state as well as build tech skills.

Any of the EduProtocols can also make great Smart Start activities with the right content. Once school is rolling along, we will want to use the EduProtocols to facilitate curriculum delivery to students. Using them from the very beginning makes sense. The key to successfully using EduProtocols for Smart Starts is the right content: fun, light, and even giggle inducing. Students can use them to build culture while learning.

Remember to use the Smart START Guiding Principles (Smile, Teach, Activities, Routines, and Target Barriers) to keep you on target as you develop activities for your students.

Individually, Smart Start activities are not necessarily mind blowing, but as a weeklong initiation into a classroom or school, they have the power to be mind shifting!

Call to Action

Refer back to the list of essential things students will need to be able to do by the end of the first week of class, which you created in Chapter 4. Look over the Smart Start activities in Chapters 5–11 and choose a few to help you meet your goals or adapt some of the EduProtocols. Keep in mind the purpose of Smart Start activities and that protocols can be used as Smart Start activities as well as preseason warm-ups.

Plan these activities and implement. If you are past the first week of school, pause your curriculum for a few days. Classroom culture will develop. The question is, will you lead its development? It's never too late to build a positive classroom culture.

*We shouldn't worry about using up the internet
in schools; we get a fresh supply every day.*

—Jon Corippo

Have you ever noticed how two-year-olds often sit next to each other, but do not play *with* each other? This normal behavior for children between the ages of two and three is called "parallel play."

Schools have traditionally expected students to learn in similar parallel but in isolated environments: fill-in-the-blank workbooks, workflows with no deviation, obsessive following of directions, and non-collaborative skill demonstration. Yet this is not the current work environment embraced by the most successful businesses, such as Google, Zappos, and REI.

Parallel learning is no longer the appropriate model for classrooms. The assembly-line model, where workers work side by side with no interaction, is over! From Marlena's daughter (who reports that poor communication hurts the office workflow) to her nephew the welder (who works with a team on the construction site) or to Jon's son (who works with a team in sales), collaboration, creativity, communication, and critical thinking (the Four Cs) are all necessary skills in today's world. And among those, creativity is the catalyst which makes the other elements richer. If form follows function, then creativity is the form.

And a most wonderful gift (*surprise!*) is that children are born creative.

But as children grow, the prospects for their creativity are dim. After decades of "parallel learning" models in our schools, creativity is on the decline.

Marlena

If we need to go shopping, the form is a store. If we need to cook, the form is a kitchen. If we want to think critically, creativity is the building that enables the critical thinking, thus making creativity the form.

According to the Torrance Tests of Creative Thinking (TTCT), this natural creativity has been steadily decreasing since 1990, with the most significant losses by third grade despite increases in IQ. The insight gained from George Land's study is that "non-creative behavior is learned," as children grow older. Creativity continues to be a concern for today's workforce. According to the *World Economic Forum: The Future of Jobs Report 2017*, here are the top job skills that students will need in 2020:

1. Complex problem-solving
2. Critical thinking
3. Creativity

Creativity was in the tenth position in the 2015 skills list, and in 2017, it's in position number three.

We have known for some time that creativity was a necessary skill for lasting success in life, yet historically we still manage to exclude it from the things we *teach* children.

We might begin to see the effects of a new and changing world on our students' lives sooner than we expected. The *Future Jobs Report* estimates that 65 percent of children entering primary schools today will ultimately work in new job types and functions that currently don't yet exist. This is a *majority* of the students in *our* classrooms today. Technological trends such as the Fourth Industrial Revolution (robotics and autonomous transport) will create many new cross-functional roles for which employees will need both technical and social and analytical skills.

Some countries are already making plans to become major players in the Fourth Industrial Revolution. According to CNN, China announced in mid-2017 that it wants to build a $150 billion AI industry by 2030. In the United States, *MIT Technology Review* explains that drones will play a large part in farming management to meet the food needs of a growing worldwide population. And according to Forbes Magazine, "smart farming" is the next hurdle for agriculture, which must increase food production by 70 percent by 2050.

With a $293.8 billion creative industry which includes entertainment, visual arts, fashion, and publishing, California is beginning to understand their economy depends on a workforce with creative strengths in addition to academic strengths. In 2017 California passed AB-37 to authorize new media arts standards for California's K–12 classrooms, which will define the creative and technological development of students while also developing skills that employers value, such as collaboration, flexibility, adaptiveness, and teamwork.

It is up to us to prepare a workforce that can tackle the challenges of this changing future.

We know that reshaping the bigger system is not practical at the teacher level. However, there are many things teachers can do in their classrooms to keep kids growing and hungry for more:

- Incorporate different kinds of creativity into your assignments and content.
- Present content to students using a variety of methods and modalities.
- Shift the bulk of the work and hard thinking to students.
- Allow students to show what they know.
- Refocus teacher attention on student learning.

Classroom Spaces

Physical space can influence the focus of a classroom, but a clear philosophy behind the instructional space is just as important. Thinking through the lens of the student experience, from the student point of view, is key to designing our school and classroom instructional space to fit the needs of the student. And considering how the instructional space should *not* look is as important as how it *should* look and feel.

I (Jon) helped open Minarets High School, a 1:1 high school, in 2008. I didn't want to make it a huge "institution of substitution" where MacBooks would be used to type the essay and do online, Scantron-style quizzes. On a road trip, another teacher and I start-

Jon

It seems the better we get at "school," the more creativity suffers. That's no way to build a nation.

It's kind of fun to do the impossible.

—Walt Disney

An Iron Chef is a jig-saw activity in a game format, in which students share the responsibility of summarizing material and reporting out to the class.

ed a conversation about how lecture and note-taking could be eliminated from our classes while still completing the academics. A rollicking five-hour conversation birthed the "Iron Chef Edu-Protocol." (We discuss how to use the Iron Chef protocol in detail in Chapter 13.)

The on-the-road design process created the criteria: timed, fast paced, and engaging. We explored TV game shows for ideas. After throwing out some failed ideas, Iron Chef appeared as the winning model. We aligned it with the tried-and-true jigsaw lesson plan with a few twists, including the use of collaborative slides. Over the years, this developed into a mindset of *plan-collaborate-deliver* where students quickly plan an approach, collaborate to create a product, and then deliver to an audience.

Plan   Collaborate   Deliver

The Iron Chef EduProtocol has a few key ingredients:

- The teacher provides the *mise en place* (a French culinary phrase meaning "putting in place" or "everything in its place") via a slide deck with the instructions in the slides.
- Each student builds a single slide in only ten minutes, including their "secret ingredient" (a self-selected, unique item to add to their slides).
- The students present their work immediately: *plan-collaborate-deliver* in action.
- The protocol shifts the main workflow from teacher-to-student to student-to-student.

The Iron Chef EduProtocol works with every grade level (we've seen it used down to second grade, using Simple Wikip—an easier-to-read version of Wikipedia) and every subject area. Teachers can eliminate the initial direct instruction with the Iron Chef EduProtocol by pointing kids to focused, high-quality resources and then letting the students report what they find. It's fun. It's loud. It's engaging. You can replace almost any lecture/note-taking classwork with this EduProtocol. And best of all, since students in Jon's classroom would do one Iron Chef a week, they had multiple opportunities to use tech in class, present, and work in a deep Four Cs-type of classroom.

This decade-long learning experience for Jon would never have occurred if he had just *worked through the workbook.*

We are the instructional space designers of our classrooms. We can design the environment we want! Once we build the culture and prove that this class will be different by embracing the Four Cs mindset, we get to work filling our instructional space with the evidence of that philosophy. In the following chapters, we will begin to develop a foundation for a new reality in your classroom—one you can replicate on your own. We will then show you how to use the EduProtocols to provide the "frames" for the instructional evidence.

Marlena

Iron Chef is a summarizing and synthesizing activity. Students use many skills in these activities; for example: when to skim text, when to close read, applying critical thinking skills, and comparing and contrasting texts.

Jon

Many teachers desire to "make it through the entire textbook" as a benchmark of academic success. But I'll bet you've never told a teacher, "Thanks for getting all the way through the textbook. It made all the difference for me this year!"

Marlena

Finished workbooks are not a demonstration of mastery. What next year's teacher wants is kids who are confident in their abilities and skills.

Call to Action

Consider the industries in your area like manufacturing, agriculture, and tech, and note how they are changing. What skills will young adults of the future need in order to navigate this new world? How might creativity (thinking outside the usual norms and pushing past the first solution that presents itself) benefit your students in *their* future?

For more about the Iron Chef lesson, please visit our website: EduProtocols.com.

Chapter 14

The Four C's Throwdown

Out of clutter, find simplicity.

—Albert Einstein

The Four Cs consist of four universal skills, identified by the Partnership for 21st Century Skills, that successful adults use every day: collaboration, creativity, communication, and critical thinking.

Collaboration: Using interpersonal and intrapersonal skills when working with *other students.*

Communication: Sharing one's work, research, and projects with other students and adults inside and outside the four walls of the classroom. This communication includes making work public to an audience beyond the classroom, generally through some form of publishing.

Critical Thinking: Students analyze problems, data, research, literature, or mathematics by solving real-world problems.

Creativity: Open-ended and choice-driven activities in which *students* have autonomy in the process and results. Often the overlap of collaboration, critical thinking, and communication creates an environment where creativity is necessary to accomplish the task so creativity can flourish.

Jon

Lecture is not a preferred form of communication in this model.

Developing a Deeper Understanding of the Four Cs

"What are we supposed to do with this again?" asked one of five principals looking at a paper describing the Four Cs.

I (Jon) looked around the room at the principals and directors who were attending the fall planning meeting. I was hoping to introduce the concept of the Four Cs to them. I replied, "These are skills that students need to develop in our classrooms. These are the skills that employers and colleges will be looking for in our kids."

They had never seen this list of soft skills, never mind the application of those skills to classroom protocols. It was, by all accounts, an entirely new way of thinking for them compared to their data-driven, benchmark system which had been developed and implemented district-wide in the past.

"How are we supposed to measure this?" asked another principal.

"I don't get what this looks like in the classroom," another one said. "Do you have examples?"

The principals continued to pepper me with questions, and I attempted to explain until the meeting came to an early end. As Marlena and I walked to our cars, I looked at Marlena and muttered, "They aren't getting it."

As the next month's meeting opened to a mixed audience of principals and teachers, I passed out a handout with the Four Cs in four boxes, in the style of a Frayer.

"Activity number one," I announced, as I pointed to the picture on the board. "Which one has more Four-C potential: the traditional paper book report or the book report video in which students summarize the book using stick puppets and post the video to their class website?"

The principals and teachers discussed the merits of each activity.

"With the video, they would have to write out the script." one principal commented. "That would be the ELA standards part."

After a long pause, a sixth-grade teacher timidly volunteered, "The acting would be high in communication."

"Ohhhh, I get it!" another teacher exclaimed.

The discussion continued between teachers and principals until the final vote. The video book report won by a landslide.

I (Marlena) glanced across the room and caught Jon's eye. The corners of his mouth barely turned upwards into a smile as he knowingly nodded and turned away. And the Four C's Throwdown was born.

As an iteration (there have been many since), I (Jon) converted the paper-pen version of the Four C's Throwdown to a Kahoot survey. I have featured the Four C's Throwdown in other countries and with groups as large as six hundred educators. Kahoot helped make the Four C's Throwdown a mass audience concept. To date, the Four C's Throwdown Kahoot has had more than 146 plays and over eight thousand players.

Marlena

I'm sure I heard Jon encourage the group, "Look beyond the standards," in his best Jedi voice. I wasn't sure if he intended to stretch out the word *beyond* to sound like Yoda, but the force was with him this day.

The Four C's Throwdown

Critical Thinking	Communication
Is there depth? *Does the activity go beyond the entry level?* (10 possible points)	*Who talks to whom?* *Is it public?* (10 possible points)

Total of 40

Collaboration	Creativity
Is there potential for students to work together with purpose? (10 possible points)	*Is it open ended?* *Is there student choice?* (10 possible points)

Total Possible Points ___ / 40

Every teacher knows that some activities facilitate deeper learning for students than others, but our judgment has become clouded by overexposure to a textbook-driven culture. Often, more profound events and experiences are also the most meaningful for students, but do we remember how to spot them? Recalibrate your thinking by taking the Four C's Throwdown quiz.

Directions

Communication: 0–10

Collaboration: 0–10

Creativity: 0–10

Critical Thinking: 0–10

Add the totals for each item and round to 0, 10, 20, or 35+

In each round of the throwdown, we will examine two different assignments. Regarding the Four Cs, the two tasks are somewhat related but not necessarily the same. Our task is to determine which assignment has the most Four Cs potential and to calibrate our sensitivity to the level of engagement in each activity. One key point to remember is that the Four C's Throwdown is not about "good" or "bad" assignments or teachers. The focus is on the Four Cs potential of the work students do. We want to recalibrate our thinking about what makes an engaging assignment for students using communication, critical thinking, creativity, and collaboration skills.

Read through each round of the throwdowns and consider the questions on the Four C's Frayer for each item.

After each round, reflect on which one you believe has a higher level of Four Cs potential. Score each of the Four Cs from zero to ten points. Add up the totals for each activity for a potential total of forty. Use the image to help you visualize the scoring.

Are you ready for the Throwdown? Here we go.

Throwdown Round 1: Literary Devices

Activity Example A: Poetry and Literary Devices

Students work alone or with a partner to identify literary devices in a poem or popular song. They then record the literary devices on the worksheet.

4 C's Score for Activity A

Communication (0-10): _____

Collaboration (0-10): _____

Creativity (0-10): _____

Critical Thinking (0-10): _____

Total Points for Activity A

(circle one) 0 10 20 35+

Poetry and Literary Devices   **Name**_____

Underline and explain the poetic device used in each line of the haikus by an unknown poet. Underline and explain the literary devices that may include: metaphors, similes, personification, hyperbole, alliteration, assonance, allusion, diction, or rhyme.

Lines	Literary Device
See light in the sky Feel like a bright star winning Brave as a lion	
Woody, my main man Rescue me, oh, rescue me Save me from myself	
I held her up high I threw her to the blue sky Up, I tossed her up	
The oceans warm breath Blows across land silently As the spring grass dies	
Lamp post sentry stands Over the walk, listening For strays to whisper	
Ask and I shall call Upon an angel awaiting Attending to our craving	

Activity Example B: Cartoon Literary Devices

4 C's Score for Activity B

Communication (0-10): _____

Collaboration (0-10): _____

Creativity (0-10): _____

Critical Thinking (0-10): _____

Total Points for Activity B

(circle one)   0   10   20   35+

Students will choose four literary devices from a list of many common literary devices and create a compilation video using clips from cartoons, songs, commercials, or movies, then label and explain the literary device in their video. Students publish the videos to a class YouTube playlist. Here's the key: Students must list why the literary device is known to be present for each device they identify, as in the image below.

Throwdown Round 2: Bill of Rights

Activity Example C: Bill of Rights Report

Each student chooses one Bill of Rights to research on their own and explain in writing. Students include images from the internet depicting their amendment.

4 C's Score for Activity C

Communication (0-10): _____

Collaboration (0-10): _____

Creativity (0-10): _____

Critical Thinking (0-10): _____

Total Points for Activity C

(circle one)   0   10   20   35+

The Bill of Rights Amendment IV
by Bobbi J. Jones

The 4th amendment in the Bill of Rights is about being able to keep your home and property secure against the police just walking in and doing what they want.

The police cannot just come in and search your home and take whatever they want. That just isn't right. You cannot be searched without a really good reason. And the police will need a search warrant to come into your house or car. The search has to be reasonable.

This amendment came about because the British soldiers would invade the colonists property without warning and the colonists did not like that.

Activity Example D: Bill of Rights Website

4 C's Score for Activity D

Communication (0-10): _____

Collaboration (0-10): _____

Creativity (0-10): _____

Critical Thinking (0-10): _____

Total Points for Activity D

(circle one)   0   10   20   35+

Inspired by Theresa Kraemer's Bill of Rights Class Website

Students, in teams, create a Bill of Rights page on a shared class website. Each team researches and creates a page explaining one amendment from the Bill of Rights. Students film and post videos of short skits explaining the amendment and create a line drawing depicting the Bill of Rights for their page. Upon completion, the students publish on the class website and share with families.

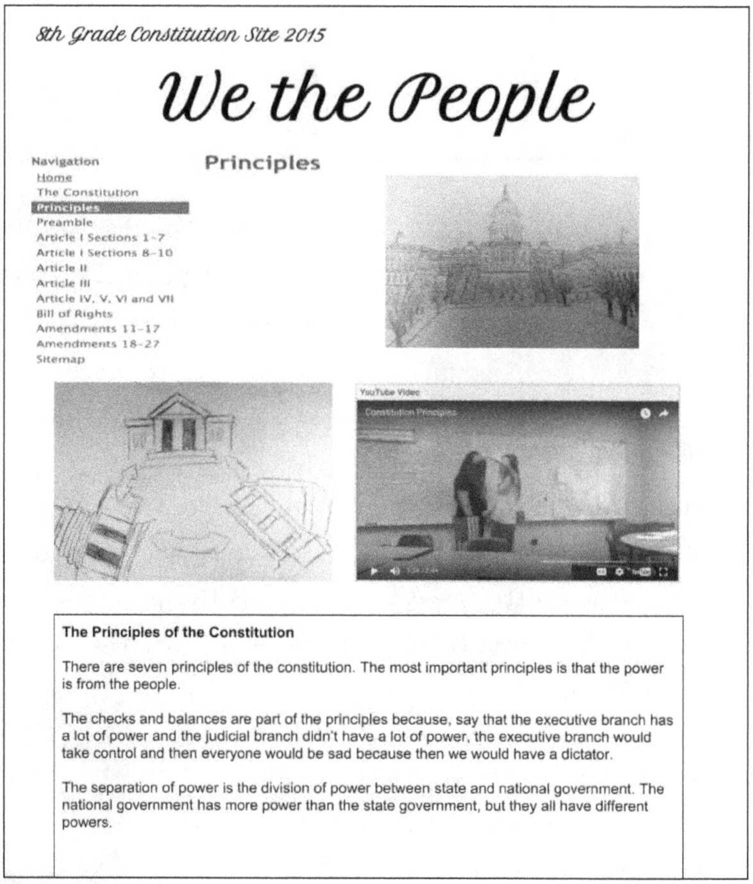

Throwdown Round 3: State History

Activity Example E: California Mission Report

As done by thousands of children all across California for what seems like generations, students learn about California history by visiting a California mission. Each student then completes a written report. The report should include information about the Native American nation in the mission vicinity, routes of colonization, daily lives in the mission, role of the Franciscans in influencing California's economy, and more (History-Social Science Content Standards for the State of California Public Schools: Grade Four 1998). Students read the report to their class. Using materials from home or purchased by parents, students build a model of the mission at home and share at open house.

4 C's Score for Activity E

Communication (0-10): _____

Collaboration (0-10): _____

Creativity (0-10): _____

Critical Thinking (0-10): _____

Total Points for Activity E

(circle one)   0   10   20   35+

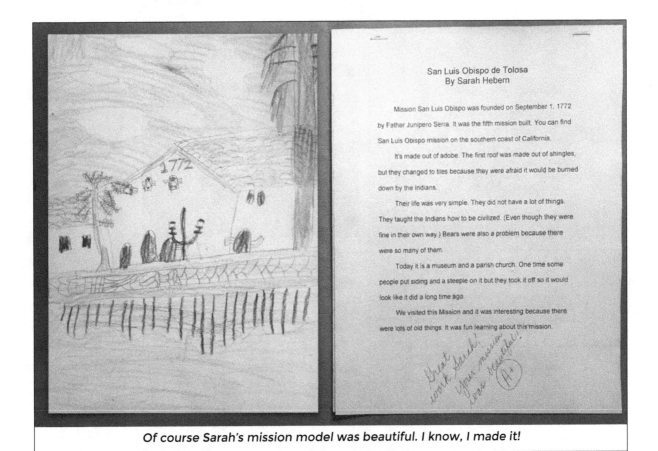

Of course Sarah's mission model was beautiful. I know, I made it!

Activity Example F: California 22nd Mission Report

4 C's Score for Activity F

Communication (0-10): _____

Collaboration (0-10): _____

Creativity (0-10): _____

Critical Thinking (0-10): _____

Total Points for Activity F

(circle one)   0   10   20   35+

Students work in groups to create a class-wide Google MyMap project for their mission reports by creating, linking, and inter-linking missions (creating one big map of everyone's content). Content includes images, student-created videos, and text. Points of interest on the map include parts of the missions, regions of the local tribes relevant to the particular mission, local resources that were critical to the success of the mission, trade routes, and more. Students are challenged to demonstrate their learning by de-signing and creating the next mission in the series. The connected maps, indicating each student's twenty-second mission (There are twenty-one California missions; students apply the knowledge they have gained thus far and design the twenty-second mission), is uploaded (using the .kml file) to the New Google Earth and shared on the internet for other students to explore.

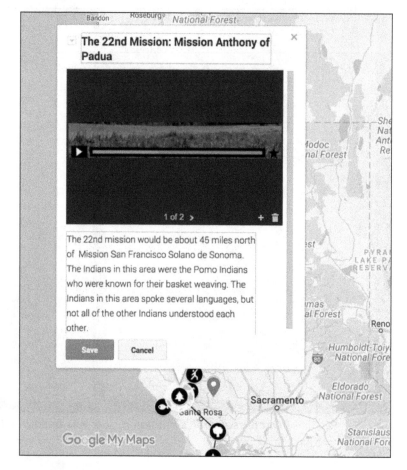

Throwdown Round 4: Math

Activity Example G: Reducing and Comparing Ratios

Students will complete a worksheet and solve for the ratio for each problem.

4 C's Score for Activity G

Communication (0-10): _____

Collaboration (0-10): _____

Creativity (0-10): _____

Critical Thinking (0-10): _____

Total Points for Activity G

(circle one)   0   10   20   35+

Reducing Ratios

Reduce each ratio to its lowest form.

Ex) 50:35	1) 49:21	2) 42:54
10:7		
3) 6:3	4) 45:20	5) 20:36
6) 12:32	7) 35:28	8) 12:8
9) 2:16	10) 15:24	11) 10:45
12) 10:70	13) 27:36	14) 80:5
15) 10:110	16) 12:36	17) 7:21
18) 42:30	19) 42:12	20) 64:72

Answers

1.
2.
3.
4.
5.
6.
7.
8.
9.
10.
11.
12.
13.
14.
15.
16.
17.
18.
19.
20.

1-10	95	90	85	80	75	70	65	60	55	50
11-30	45	40	35	30	25	20	15	10	5	0

Activity Example H: Mullet Ratio

4 C's Score for Activity H

Communication (0-10): _____

Collaboration (0-10): _____

Creativity (0-10): _____

Critical Thinking (0-10): _____

Total Points for Activity H

(circle one)   0   10   20   35+

Created by: Matt Vaudrey and John Stevens, *The Classroom Chef*

After learning to identify a mullet haircut and studying and discussing the merits of different types of mullets to determine which is the most "mullet-y," students use the party in back : business in front ratio to compare haircuts with one another. This lesson unfolds like this, according to Matt Vaudrey in *The Classroom Chef*: "We'd been comparing mullets for twenty minutes, during which no math was done, no paper was used, and no numbers were seen. Only after we needed the math did we bring it in. That's what it means to need the math to serve the conversation."

The Mullet Ratio

$$R_m = \frac{\text{Party}}{\text{Business}}$$

$$R_m = \frac{17cm}{9cm}$$

$$R_m = 1.\overline{8}$$

Four C's Throwdown Reflection

Our task in this chapter was to calibrate our thinking about lesson design by determining which assignment types had the most Four C *potential*. Not all tasks will necessarily incorporate all the Four Cs, nor will all of them have the same level of potential for Four C engagement. But each one should reflect some aspect of the Four Cs in more than one area.

Look for keywords that indicate Four C potential:

Collaboration	Creativity
Groups	Create
Partners	Build
Whole class	Design
Connect to an outside source	Original
Expert	
Discuss	

Communication	Critical Thinking
Share	Demonstrate
Present	Describe
Publish	Connect
Display	Synthesize
Explain	Critique
	Prove
	Analyze
	Organize
	Compare

Marlena

Just looking for the one word is not enough! Look to see what other words follow the keyword; for example, sharing with a partner is much different from sharing online.

Note: *We've bolded words we have keyed into as clues to help us focus on the Four Cs potential.*

Our comments are not intended to indicate right or wrong answers to readers, but rather as insight into our thinking about what we liked and didn't like about these activities.

What do we think about these activities?

In the following section, we share our thoughts about the Four C's Throwdown activities.

Activity Example A: Poetry and Literary Devices

Collaboration: 0–10
depending if partners are in play

Communication: 0

Critical Thinking: 5

Creativity: 0

Students work alone or with a partner to identify literary devices in a poem or popular song. They record the literary device on the **worksheet**.

Our thoughts: Don't be deceived by this one! It seems fun when the content is something the kids can relate to, such as a well-liked song; however, it is still just a worksheet.

Activity Example B: Cartoon Literary Devices

Collaboration: 0–10
if partners are in play

Communication: 0–5
if students comment on each other's videos

Critical Thinking: 10

Creativity: 10

Students **create a compilation** video about literary devices by using clips from cartoons, songs, commercials, or movies, then label and **explain the literary device** in the video and **publish** to their YouTube playlist. Students choose four literary devices from a list of many and then **find** accompanying clips. Here's the key: They must list **why** the literary device is known to be present.

Our thoughts: This open-ended activity allows for a significant degree of student choice and voice which ups the creativity factor. Learning how to put the video together and finding the right clips for the literary device takes analyzing and thinking skills to the next level.

Activity Example C: Bill of Rights Report

Each student chooses one Bill of Rights to **research on their own, then explains in writing**. Students **include** images from the internet depicting their amendment.

Our thoughts: Research is important, but is it meaningful to kids? Research alone is probably not personal enough to engage students for long since this is a common activity they've done for years. Seventh and eighth graders are ready for much more. Also, collaboration is a missed opportunity with this activity.

Collaboration: 0

Communication: 0

Critical Thinking: 10

Creativity: 5

Activity Example D: Bill of Rights Website

Students **form teams** to create a Bill of Rights page on a **shared class website**. Each team **researches and creates** a page **explaining** one amendment from the Bill of Rights. **Students film** short skits **explaining** the amendment and **post the videos on the website**. Students **create line drawing** images depicting the Bill of Rights for their page. Upon completion, the **students publish** the website and **share with families**.

Our thoughts: What we love about this project is its simplicity. Deep Four Cs engagement does not have to be overly complicated. The line drawings and the videos without backgrounds and props serve the purpose to engage kids. It accomplishes the Four C's potential without unnecessary pageantry.

Collaboration: 1–10

Communication: 10

Critical Thinking: 10

Creativity: 10

Activity Example E: California Mission Report

Collaboration: 10

Communication: 10

Critical Thinking: 0–10
depending on the parents'
involvement in the project

Creativity: 0–10
depending on the parents'
involvement in the project

Students **learn about** California history by visiting and researching a California mission. Each student **completes a written report.** The report should include information about the Native American nation in the mission vicinity, routes of colonization, daily lives in the mission, role of the Franciscans in influencing California's economy, and more. (History–Social Science Content Standards for the State of California Public Schools: Grade Four 1998) **Students read the report to their class**. Using materials from home or purchased by parents, **students build** a model of the mission **at home** and share at Open House.

Our thoughts: If you live outside of California and are not familiar with the notorious Mission Model Project, you might mistake this as requiring a high level of creativity. However, in most cases, it is well known that parents experience the most creativity in this activity.

Marlena

I'm embarrassed to admit that I helped way too much, since the complicated mission design was beyond my fourth grader. Fix the parent takeover by scaffolding up to large projects kids can do on their own or sizing projects down for independence.

Activity Example F: California 22nd Mission Report

Collaboration: 10

Communication: 10

Critical Thinking: 10

Creativity: 10

Students work in groups to create a class-wide Google My-Map project for their mission reports by **creating and linking,** and **intralinking** missions (creating one big map of everyone's content). Content includes images, and **student-created** videos and text. Points of interest on the map included parts of the missions, regions of the local tribes relevant to the particular mission, local resources that were critical to the success of the mission, trade routes, and more. Students are challenged to **demonstrate their learning** by **designing and creating the next mission** in the series. The connected maps, including each student's 22nd mission (a mission **they create**), is uploaded (using the .kml file) to the New Google Earth and **shared on the internet for other students to explore.**

Our Thoughts: This certainly changes up a traditional project. The linked maps take collaboration to the next level. Fourth graders can accomplish this project without parental help. The New Google Earth brings this project to life, but what we love the most about this project is that, regardless of format, the mission reports live online long past the lifespan of the cardboard models.

Activity Example G: Reducing Ratios

Students will complete a worksheet and solve for the ratio for each problem.

Our thoughts: Another worksheet? Enough said.

Collaboration: 0

Communication: 0

Critical Thinking: 5

Creativity: 0

Activity Example H: Mullet Ratio

After learning to identify a mullet haircut and studying and **discussing the merits** of different types of mullets to determine which is the most "mullet-y," students use the party in back : business in front **ratio to compare haircuts** with one another. In *The Classroom Chef*, Matt Vaudrey explains how the lesson unfolds: "We'd been comparing mullets for twenty minutes, during which no math was done, no paper was used, and no numbers were seen. Only after **we needed the math** did we bring it in. That's what it means to need the **math to serve** the conversation."

Our thoughts: Matt Vaudrey completely flips the activity so that the math drives the discussion further, developing an opening for students to use a high level of critical thinking skills as applied to a real-world problem to make sense of the information they seek. Not only do students develop a sense of wonder about

Collaboration: 10

Communication: 0

Critical Thinking: 10

Creativity: 10
(depending on how the math evolves)

solving their problem, Vaudrey has also created a setting where students need math.

Call to Action

Jon encouraged principals and teachers to "Look *beyond* the standards."

As you reflect on the communication, critical thinking, creativity, and collaboration skills used in your classroom, consider the following questions as you look beyond the standards:

- How might the Four Cs be more deeply incorporated into students' learning?

- How might existing program materials be modified to include Four C's skill development for my students?

- How might incorporating more Four Cs into my classroom affect student perception of experiences?

- How might these skills and keywords in the chart be used to support standards mastery in my classroom?

You may not have all the answers today, and that is quite okay. In the chapters of this book, you will find many tools and techniques to incorporate the Four Cs more efficiently. But the ways to incorporate the Four Cs are not limited to the pages of this book. Only our imagination limits the possibilities! There is no one single method, process, or trick. Knowing your students—that's what will help you look for openings in your curriculum where you can sneak in some Four C's skills.

Just remember, many students are not accustomed to working this way and may need guidance and structure to get started. As with growing capacity, it's all about the reps.

With time, they will get better at it, and so will you! May the Four Cs be with you.

EduProtocols

Chapter 15

Creativity in the Hands of Kids

When we try to pick out anything by itself, we find
it hitched to everything else in the Universe.

—John Muir

We absolutely love helping students work together to learn and explore content. Educational researcher of cognitive and high-yield teaching strategies, Robert J. Marzano, identified the importance of cooperative learning, placing it sixth on his list of Nine Essential Instructional Strategies.

In our classrooms, we see that when students are working in groups, the level of creativity increases. They bounce ideas off one another and develop new ideas they would not have thought of on their own. The EduProtocols use the strengths of collaboration and creativity to facilitate a deeper understanding of content. With planning and structure that allows students to focus on collaboration, the creative payoff is huge!

Our EduProtocols include the following features to enable the most bang for the buck!

Jon

When designing EduProtocols which feature collaboration, it's critical to avoid the common pitfalls shown below.

1. Workload Equity

One pitfall of traditional group work is kids not sharing the work equitably. (*He did everything! She did nothing!*) Handle this problem with clear and discrete tasks performed by each individual. It's tricky to design, but critical. Happily, once you establish a we-all-work culture, the demand for correction lessens during the year. The key is for each student to be accountable for one piece of the work without letting that piece destroy the whole work (see Iron Chef).

2. Cooperative vs. Collaborative

Our goal should not be mere cooperation, which is where most classic "group work" falls. Our highest goal should be collaboration. Check out John Spencer's epic graphic which shows the differences:

Some of the activities in the following chapters are higher in the cooperative range, and some are higher in the collaborative range. Both skills are essential for students to practice and develop.

Front-load tech skills to focus workflows on content.

3. Prepare Students to Work with Slides

It will be easier for students to build the slides in the following activities if they first complete the "Worst Preso EVER" activity in Chapter 2. While this is not a prerequisite, completing this fun slide deck will front-load students in their ability to create slides and will help to streamline workflow, keeping the focus on content and boosting self-confidence. Chapter 2 contains suggestions for littles as well.

4. Slide Type:
Report Slide vs. Presentation Slide
(Also Known as Thin and Thick Slides)

We use two types of slides with students as part of their collaborative projects. One is a "thin" slide in a presentation style, where images dominate. You would expect to see this type of slide in a presentation where the speaker primarily tells the story.

The "thick" slide uses more text than images and can be used as a mini-paper, research report, research notepad, or documentation-type project. You would expect to see this format when the slide acts as the presenter since it contains more information than a typical slide. Use it as an easy way for students to share their learnings.

Jon

Think of a Thick Preso slide as a deconstructed paragraph containing all the things kids would need for an effective paragraph in a single slide: maybe half a dozen facts (tabling them is a nice option), two or three sources, two or three pictures, and a couple of quotes.

Presentation Slide v. Report Slide

- Title
- Eye-catching image or graphic
- Speaker tells the story

- Two sources
- Informative

- 2-3 Pictures with captions
- Table to compare 3-4 facts
- 1st person quote
- 3rd person quote
- Slide tells story

Ceasar's Political History

Both types of slides have a purpose when used with students, depending on the goals and the task assigned. Several of the activities below will use "thick" slides, even when students are presenting.

5. Cognitive Load: How Much Is Too Much?

We want to keep the cognitive load low as we introduce students to new workflows. We recommend using light, fun content the first two times in which an EduProtocol is run.

Cori Orlando shares her experience with how much is too much, and what happens when the cognitive load exceeds the patience of learners:

Plot twist! We need to stop for a minute. There I was, standing in front of twenty of my peers, sharing my fail in real time. This was not one of my normal fails: This was a fail of epic proportions. Why? Well, because I had just done something in my professional development session that I had warned teachers not to do with their students!

Whenever I show educators a new tool, strategy, or protocol, I always give the same disclaimer. On this particular day, I went so far as to have an actual slide devoted to it (with a photo of caution tape). My fear was that if they didn't get it, things would go awry in their classroom, and that particular tool, strategy, or protocol would go back on the shelf, never to be tried again.

Here is my plea: Whenever introducing a new tool, strategy, or protocol to your students, start with a very low cognitive load. Please! What does that mean? It means wrap it around content that is easy, fun, and familiar to your students. Something like Disneyland, food, superheroes, and mullets. Since the tool, strategy, or protocol is something you will be using repeatedly with your class, you want the focus on the technology skills at first. With a low cognitive load, students can expend their brain power to create. After many successful repetitions, you can ramp up the content.

If students are given a completely new task—and unfamiliar or difficult content—something is going to get lost. They either lose out on the tool, activity, protocol, or the content. Sometimes, all of it. What are you left with? Frustrated students and a frustrated you.

Here is the example from that professional development session: I gave participants a choice board with different tools to explore with the content of "Little Red Riding Hood and the Big Bad Wolf." This is a familiar story, so they were able to spend their time and energy on creating, using the tools. (They had a blast with this!) I usually give participants the content of "Little Red Riding Hood," but on this particular day I decided to change that content to the "Hero's Journey," which was one of the themes of the conference. They had already watched a short video that morning about the Hero's Journey, and I figured everyone knew the premise. Low cognitive load, right? Wrong. During the "creating time," I observed people re-watching the video and researching the content—with a lot of distress and some sweat. What I didn't observe was people digging into the tools.

Plot twist. Time to adjust course.

I stopped them. I called attention to my mistake, and we discussed the issue. They were actually able to feel, first hand, what happens when you give a new task with a higher cognitive load. We took it back a notch. I gave them the "Little Red Riding Hood" prompt, and with a sigh of relief, they began to dig in.

I have had teachers confide in me that they have tried something that I had showed them, but it "didn't go well" and they were afraid to try it again. "It took too long. The students didn't understand the content; they just messed around with the tools."

My first question is always What was the content? *The answer is usually something regarding whatever subject they were teaching at the time, like "comparing and contrasting ancient Egypt to present Egypt." At that point, I imagine children's heads exploding from overload.*

As you begin planning out your use of protocols, use my cautionary tale to remind yourself to take it slow at first; don't jump straight in with content. I know it's hard, because it is exciting to try something new. And I know how we always feel pressed for time. We think, "Let's just do it!" But I promise you, time on the front end will pay dividends on the back end. Once the students become comfortable with the protocol, the protocol becomes second nature and moves to the back of their minds. This opens up space for the content to move to the front, which is the ultimate goal.

And in the end, if it doesn't go well, just say, "Plot twist!" and try it again tomorrow.

Here We Go!

The activities in the following chapters are ones we most enjoy sharing with students. They are all wonderfully structured to incorporate the Four Cs as students work through the challenges presented in each type of activity. All of them can be used with any subject and modified for a broad range of grade levels.

Students use the Frayer, created by Dorothy Frayer and her colleagues at the University of Wisconsin, to develop a deeper understanding of vocabulary. It can also be applied to other concepts in subjects such as math, science, and history.

Definition	Characteristics
An amazing revelation or insight that is sudden.	Sudden Revelation Ah-ha moment

Epiphany

Example	Non-Example
David realized that his grand idea would solve all of his problems!	Joshua had absolutely no idea what to do next. He was completely clueless.

Note: We find that computer drawing programs (especially Google Draw, PowerPoint 365, or Keynote in iCloud) lend themselves wonderfully to creating Frayers.

Academic Goals

- Develop understanding of words or concepts.
- Create a simple graphic organizer that students can replicate on their own.
- Make learning and memorizing attainable when appropriate.

Teacher Big Ideas

- Fast
- Easy to replicate
- Facilitates deeper under-standings

Prepare for the Activity

Prepare the Frayer model in an electronic format. (Frayer may also be used on paper.)

Instructions

Step 1: Provide a copy of the electronic Frayer to each student or pairs of students (if working in teams). Frayers are commonly used individually, but may be used with partners where collaboration and conversation can extend the value of concept construction among students.

Step 2: Students complete the Frayer using words and images.

Key Points to Remember

- Finding the right images for a Frayer is delightfully complicated. Many words do not have direct corresponding images; for example, *diligently*. Students must find an image that shows "diligently." Typing this word into the image search will often not result in pictures that are useful. Students must think of another search term that will illustrate the meaning of the word.
- The best example for the non-example uses something that is easily confused with the word, but not the same; for example, *fork* (utensil). Here it might be "pitchfork," whereas a very easy Google search for an antonym will result in the words, *converge*, *join*, and *branch* and does not necessarily deepen the understanding of the use of fork in this example.

Adapting for Littles

- Allow littles to rely on images more than text alone. Frayers can be either complicated or simple based on the word that is featured on each Frayer.

Chapter 17

BookaKucha EduProtocol

Are you looking for a different way to hold students accountable for their personal reading? Tired of outdated online assessments for reading comprehension? Are your students completing book reports at different times, creating a bookkeeping headache? With BookaKucha, everyone stops and completes a four-slide book report at the same time, regardless of the page number!

The traditional PechaKucha presentation consists of twenty slides that automatically advance in twenty-second intervals, creating a mini-TED-talk effect that keeps the speaker moving. PechaKucha events have gained world-wide popularity after the first one took place in Tokyo in February 2003. We can harness the fun of the PechaKucha for book reports.

Academic Goals

- Foster interest in peer-reviewed books and a class culture of reading.
- Practice presenting in a concise and systematic manner.
- Include weekly or bi-weekly comprehension reflections.

Teacher Big Ideas

- BookaKucha brings a component of both book talks and lit circles to book reports.
- Finding one conflict or element in a book is easy; identifying two more is the challenge!
- Presentations are easy to grade and manage in real time.
- Fast presentations: A one-minute (three slides at twenty seconds each) presentation per student should take about a forty-minute class period, or less, for the entire class to present and be graded.
- ALL students complete a BookaKucha once weekly or bi-monthly to develop fluency and to ensure exploration of a wide variety of book themes.

Description

Ideally, in a class of thirty, each student will be reading a book of their choice at any given time, but it can be difficult to hold thirty different students in thirty different books accountable for reading. This activity is designed so that each student develops their own book report at the same time as their classmates, regardless of the page number the student is reading. Everybody pauses the reading at the same time, develops four slides based on where they are in the book at that moment, and presents three of the slides within a one-minute snapshot (three slides at twenty seconds each). This allows the teacher to grade everyone in about one period and encourages a culture of reading in the classroom. Done regularly (weekly or bi-weekly), the BookaKucha provides a format to easily document student reading progress while helping students to analyze their own reading at a deeper level.

For this activity, the teacher chooses a theme for the BookaKucha book reports; for example, each student creates a report-style (thick slide) slide deck based on . . .

Three different settings in the book

- Or three different characters
- Or three important events
- Or three conflicts within the book.

Any literature theme such as character analysis, morals of the story, plot, or setting will work well for this protocol. Remember to choose just one of these themes at a time.

Example: Using *Wonder*, by R. J. Palacio, a student will identify three conflicts within the book:

- Slide One—Title Slide: name of the book, author, illustrator, student's name, and number of the last page read
- Slide Two—Conflict 1: man (Auggie) against himself (a facial deformity)
- Slide Three—Conflict 2: man (Auggie) against the world
- Slide Four—Conflict 3: man (Auggie) against man (Julian, antagonist)

Each slide would explain the lead-up and details of the conflict.

Students would present slides two through four to the class in a quick, one-minute presentation. The presentations are intended to be a snapshot of the reading and the thinking behind the development of the slides.

Prepare for the Activity

Step 1: Choose a theme for this round's BookaKucha.

Below are some suggestions for three side presentations:

- three characters
- three lessons learned
- three wishes the characters would make and why
- three settings in detail and why the setting is important to the story
- three conflicts from the following themes: man vs. nature, man vs. society, man vs. self, man vs. man, man vs. reality, or man vs. god

Step 2: Develop a blank template for students indicating what kind of information will be included on the slide.

Instructions

Step 1: Students create their presentation using this format:

Slide 1: Student name, current page number, and a bibliography-type citation that includes name of book, author, and other relevant citation information

Slide 2: One image and description

Slide 3: One image and description

Slide 4: One image and description

Step 2: Students build their slides.

Students will include quotes and text evidence to support their claim and cite the page number as reference.

Tip: Any theme or discussion questions from lit circles could be used here.

Step 3: Students present only slides two, three, and four, with each slide automatically advancing after twenty seconds. (Three slides at twenty seconds each equals a one-minute presentation.)

Step 4: Grade presentations in real time using a rubric and provide immediate feedback to students.

Steven McGriff, instructional designer, suggests one "I wonder" and two "Hallelujah" statements to frame feedback, providing one growth point and two positive praises for students.

Variations

- Allow two to three students reading the same book to develop a shared BookaKucha.
- Make choosing the literary device a fun event. Let a student draw it from a hat or spin a spinner to determine the theme of the week.
- The following week, students add to their existing slide deck rather than begin a new one. Rotate by month, quarter, or by the book so that one book is in one slide deck.

Key Points to Remember

- Introduce BookaKucha slowly (e.g., one to two slides from a shared book until kids understand the protocol).
- Pause the reading to allow students time to think about their reading.
- This activity is a snapshot and over time; snapshots reflect growth.
- To record growth, consider archiving randomly selected weeks in student portfolios for comparison over the course of the year.
- The template may be built by the teacher to guide the students, but let the students do the work of building content.

Marlena

Keep the feedback quick. I just pull students to the side and have a one-minute "conference" with them. Over time, they get better. It doesn't take much encouragement to inspire improvement.

- Older students may do well with an outline instead of a template.
- Remember that the first attempts will be lacking but will improve over the following weeks.

Adapting for Littles

- Shorten the slide deck. One slide with one image, and a short "sharing" of the book is enough.
- Provide a few images at the beginning for students to choose from. The image does not need to match the book; for example, using an image of Marc Brown's *Arthur* character is not necessary. Encourage children to look for an image that represents the book's big ideas.
- Be flexible on the time and don't advance the slides too abruptly. The goal for younger students is standing up in front of a screen and talking while facing the audience. Using paper notes with one or two key points is acceptable.
- Immediate feedback is imperative for student growth.

Tip: When a student presents a slide in five seconds, don't forward to the next slide. Wait the full, twenty seconds so the student will eventually learn the timing of twenty-second intervals. Eventually, we want the student to fill the time allotted.

Shared writing inspires stories, and stories are fun to write!
But have you ever considered creating a class math or history textbook, complete with diagrams and samples? Class books can span the grade levels and subjects. The iBook textbook, *Math Our Way*, by the students of Mr. Smith, Mr. Black, and Mr. Lehotay, is a great example of a shared content book.

The idea for fiction class books was originally developed from my (Marlena's) experience teaching kindergarten many years ago. We started with the model of a repetitive story such as *Five Little Monkeys Jumping on the Bed* by Eileen Christelow. Then each student recreates a page using their own idea for the extension of the story. The students loved creating the books and loved reading them in the class library. At the end of the year, each student would take home one of the books.

We love this protocol because using a slide format allows for a wide variety of standards-aligned topics in any grade, and the books are easily published in a class website, creating a virtual class library.

Academic Goals

- Enjoy literature together or expand understanding of a content area.
- Collaborate on a class project that can be shared.
- Write, write, write.

Teacher Big Ideas

- Divide up chapters or pages with groups of students.
- Use slides and images as an easy introduction to making slide decks.
- Scaffold research for students by providing web links or materials for the content of the book.
- If your platform allows, encourage constructive comments within the slide deck.

Description

Students create a class book using a slide deck. Each student writes one page or one part of the book. Or two students write a section together.

Prepare for the Activity

Step 1: Decide on a starter prompt or question to get kids thinking.

Step 2: Create a class slide deck, (or decks for smaller groups), with enough slides for each student.

Step 3: Share the slide deck with students.

Instructions

Step 1: Write.

Step 2: Publish.

Step 3: Present.

Key Points to Remember

- Use as a class-wide collaborative activity for any subject.
- Post finished products where students can enjoy again and again.
- Yearlong books (like a math book) makes for rich learning opportunities.

Adapting for Littles

- Use a story stem. For example: Using the book, *To Be a Kid*, by Maya Ajmera and John D. Ivanko, students write a slide finishing the line, "To be a kid means to . . . "
- Use your class anthology for ideas for one-line story stems. Students can choose or take pictures to illustrate their line.
- Use social studies/history, math, or science as starters for an informative class book.

Other Story Stems to Try

- *One Hundred is a Family* by Pam Muñoz Ryan
- Students write "Four is a family that goes camping together." And then tell about their adventure camping, or whatever it is they do together with their families.
- *If You Give a Mouse a Cookie* by Laura Numeroff
- Cori Orlando has students take pictures of items in the classroom as a starting point for their contribution.

Chapter 19

Great American Race EduProtocol

The Great American Race EduProtocol was developed by Ben Johnson, media specialist, and it has quickly become a favorite! Imagine a class, highly focused on searching online and reading with barely a sound except the tapping of keyboards or a deep breath for fear of losing precious seconds. That is the Great American Race!

Note: *If your country or origin is outside the USA, make this race your own! The Great Canadian Race, or The Great Netherlands Race, or The Great Country of Mexico Race. You pick!*

Description

In this activity, students anonymously contribute a slide to a class deck (facts, information, or vocabulary). Then, in the second half of the activity, teams race to identify each slide. Using the states as an example, students create a slide with clues for a particular state. After the deck is complete, students race to backwards research to determine the state for each slide. This activity works best with information that links directly to a title or name; for example, the periodic table, states, or California missions. Use it to introduce a new unit of study, to support "investigations," to learn about something new, or to review material.

- The Heidelberg Project was started here.
- Barry Gordy started Motown, studio A, in the garage of a little house.
- There are many deserted buildings and homes in one of the major cities in this state.
- The white-tailed deer became the state animal in 1997 after a fourth-grade class campaigned for it.
- Ford started making cars here and developed the process of the assembly line.

Studio A

The Heidelberg Project: A Community Art Project

Prepare for the Activity

Step 1: Decide on content to be covered.

These are some topic suggestions that work well with the Great American Race:

- States of the U.S.A.
- Capitals of the states
- State or U.S. history
- Missions
- Great figures in U.S. history
- Explorers
- Periodic table of elements
- Math concepts demonstrated or explained
- Careers, occupations, jobs
- Types of trees, plants, animals, bacteria, cells
- Branches of the government
- Articles of the U.S. Constitution
- Key people in the government

Step 2: Create a "key" for the slides.

Step 3: Create a way for students to submit their answers electronically via a quiz program, such as Google Forms, to save you time.

Step 4: Write each slide answer on 3x5 cards. Be sure to number the cards.

Step 5: Create a blank slide deck that is numbered and corresponds to the 3x5 cards.

Instructions

Step 1: Distribute the 3x5 cards, one to each student. "Don't show anyone your card!"

Step 2: Students find the slide with the matching number that is on the 3X5 card and develop a slide with clues to the answer on the card.

Academic Goals

- Ensure it will be student directed.
- Practice research skills (both in developing the slide and in identifying the slides).
- Organize and work using written communication.

Teacher Big Ideas

- Teach researching skills and then let students do the "heavy lifting."
- Sit back and facilitate.
- Keep it fun.

#6

Add clues about your state here:

1.

2.

3.

4.

5.

Insert image here

Once the class slide deck is complete . . .

Step 3: Create teams of two to four students.

Step 4: Students share a document or spreadsheet through which all members of the team can communicate. Number the document (e.g., 1–20).

Step 5: Students work together to research and figure out the answer to each slide. They do not talk during this process; in fact, sitting across the room from each other is helpful. Students communicate through the shared document, document chat, and comment features.

Step 6: Teacher records the order in which the teams complete the challenge.

Step 7: Check the answers. Deduct points for incorrect answers. Declare the winning team!

Variation

David Saunders, a middle school library media specialist, shares his version of *The Amazing Race* using Google Earth and My Maps:

The Amazing Race activity is a powerful way to get small teams working together in an effort to complete challenges and cross the finish line first! While there are many different ways to create Amazing Race lessons, I've most frequently used a combination of custom Google My Maps, Google Forms, and a series of challenges that happen in the digital and analog realm. Races can be used to introduce new concepts and tools, reinforce content material, and encourage collaboration and teamwork with students and colleagues.

I created a Race for the Google Geo Teacher Institute in Mountain View, California that was focused on Google Earth and Google My Maps. My objective was to provide an opportunity for participants to explore some of the new features of these tools while also working together to solve a series of mostly geographical challenges. It was important for me to develop challenges that pushed the participants into using the tools in ways that they otherwise may not have considered. For example, one of the challenges begins with a simple Google-able question: "How many countries/territories border Spain?" Armed with the answer, participants were then asked to compare the populations for each and identify the country/territory with the smallest population. Then using Google Earth, they were to locate the highest point and use Street View to explore the perspective. Using the compass tool, they then had to find true North and identify the Spanish town that lay directly over the border. Finally, they used Earth to find the elevation of that town. Once they had discovered the answer to this challenge, they submitted a Google Form that provided them with a link to the next one!

The Amazing Race has always been a fun, high-engagement activity that I can count on to move the ball down the court.

Key Points to Remember

- Make the key first.
- Prep everything ahead.
- To keep opposing teams from eavesdropping and stealing answers, students communicate within the document, thus forcing effective written communication.

- Scale back the scaffolding on the slide template and allow students to format their own as students become familiar with the protocol.

Adapting for Littles

- Try using a textbook or other book as source material to research places in our community, career, or other topics.
- Use simple, familiar concepts so students can be successful. This can include making a slide centered around a classmate or a favorite food, places on a map, "All About Me," or "Guess My Partner."
- Remember to check over the slide deck before releasing it to the class.
- Don't focus on "a" winner. Focus on the process and the success of finding the answers.
- Use slides as a "drawing" platform and have students demonstrate concepts in math
  - Draw 7 + 4.
  - Create a number story to go along with the equation.
  - The race would be to find the answers to those equations.

Chapter 20

Cyber Sandwich EduProtocol

Students can easily copy facts from Wikipedia and create reports in minutes, but how do we move students out of the copy/paste cycle? We create different models that make the copy/paste irrelevant.

Description

In this EduProtocol, students will work in the two highest levels of Marzano's Nine Essential Instructional Strategies list from the book *Classroom Instruction That Works: Research-Based Strategies for Increasing Student Achievement.* As students record notes, compare and contrast topics, and summarize, they will begin to develop the foundational skills that can later be used to produce longer research reports and learn to digest challenging information.

Prepare for the Activity

Step 1: Choose two aspects of one category to compare and contrast. (We used nineteenth-century news and modern-day news in our example below.) Look for items that have both similarities and differences; for example, nineteenth century vs. modern day.

Students collaborate.

Academic Goals

- Compare and contrast two like or unlike topics.
- Develop skills that can be used later in larger writing projects.
- Move students out of the copy/paste cycle.

Teacher Big Ideas

- Create *one* summary paragraph which includes differences, similarities, and a conclusion.
- Start very simple, with a narrow focus.
- Expand to multiple categories as student skills grow.
- Different teams of students might focus on comparing various categories so that presentations cover a wider range in the class as a whole.

Teaching Tip: *In our nineteenth-century news vs. modern-day news sample, the answers were not easily Google-able. Students had to think about what they knew about the time period to figure out what they were looking for in their search.)*

Category: News

Modern Day

- TV, radio, computer, social media (e.g., Twitter)
- News travels around the world very quickly

Nineteenth Century

- Printing press
- No TV
- Limited transportation, trains, horses, few cars

Compare

- News was significant in both time periods

Contrast

- Nineteenth-century printed newspapers and spread news by word-of-mouth
- The news took time to spread due to slow means of travel

Task: Create a summary paragraph that includes differences, similarities, and a conclusion.

Step 2: Create a document similar to the example. Slide one should include the question to be answered or information to be researched along with links to the two sources or texts to be compared.

Instructions

Step 1: Student One will spend ten minutes researching Topic One while Student Two does the same with Topic Two. Both students will enter their findings on Slide One.

Step 2: Students will spend five minutes discussing their findings with their partner and completing a Venn diagram together on Slide Two.

Step 3: Using the shared research and Venn diagram, *each* student will write his or her *own* paragraph comparing and

Cyber Sandwich

Step 1:
Directions: Research your topic. Record your findings from your research.

Student 1: For news in the 19th-century, click HERE for the article.

Student 2: For news from modern-day, click HERE for the article.

Cyber Sandwich

Step 2:
Directions: Research your part of the Cyber Sandwich, then work with your partner to complete the Venn diagram.

19th Century News vs. Modern News

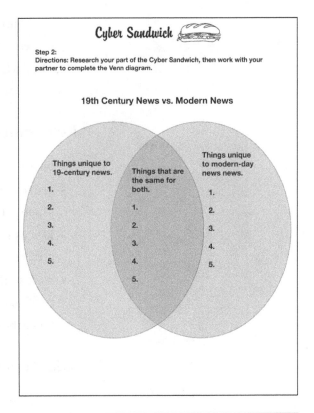

Things unique to 19-century news.
1.
2.
3.
4.
5.

Things that are the same for both.
1.
2.
3.
4.
5.

Things unique to modern-day news news.
1.
2.
3.
4.
5.

Cyber Sandwich

Student 1 Name:

Step 3:
Directions: Write a summary what you learned here. Compare news in the 19th-century with news in the modern-day.

Cyber Sandwich

Student 2 Name:

Step 3:
Directions: Write a summary what you learned here. Compare news in the 19th-century with news in the modern-day.

contrasting the two topics based on the information gathered on the slides.

Step 4: Each team will take turns presenting their findings to the class, other groups, or a partner.

Key Points to Remember

- New is messy. Proficiency builds over time.
- Narrow the focus, as the students are writing one-paragraph summaries.
- It is okay to expand the categories as student proficiency increases.
- Start simple: hamburgers vs. tacos, chocolate ice cream vs. pie, rock vs. country.
- Once the tech and protocol are mastered, build up.

Adapting for Littles

Comparing the literature that students are reading makes an ideal starting point:

- The book character vs. the movie character
- An item in the book vs. an item in real life
- Two things (e.g., car vs. carriage, cat vs. dog)
- Two processes (e.g., how we behave in the classroom vs. the playground)

Chapter 21

Internet Scavenger Hunt EduProtocol

I (Marlena) am always amazed at the things other people find on the internet. I often wonder to myself, *How did they find that?* When I Google that, I get nothing worth using! Then I discovered there are better ways to search than "What is" questions. Students often fall into the same trap when they turn to Google to find information or to answer a question, but they don't necessarily know how to use Google to find exactly what they need. Do you?

Description

Hone student search skills with an internet scavenger hunt. When a Google search is conducted, Google will indicate the number of websites returned: the lower the number, the more detailed the search terms. Students race to search for specific information on the internet and record their search results.

Students find the required information, summarize their findings, screenshot the Google search results page to show the number of returned searches, and include the screenshot on their slide. Bonus points are

Academic Goals

- Students practice and develop research skills.
- Students explore content on their own.
- Students work in teams to complete the task.

Teacher Big Ideas

- The goal is for students to practice searching for specific information.
- Work in teams to collect evidence together.

awarded to the student or team with the lowest number for each slide with the correct information.

Prepare for the Activity

Step 1: Select a topic to be researched.

Step 2: Pre-research the topic and make sure the information you are asking students to find actually exists, and that it is appropriate for students to access.

Step 3: Create the criteria students will be searching; for example, George Washington stopped his army's rebellion by putting on a pair of glasses. What was the name of the conspiracy behind the rebellion? (The search could look like this: Washington +rebellion +army +glasses.)

Note that while the second article is Wikipedia, the first is a reputable article from History.com and the number of results returned was only twenty-five.

Step 4: Prepare a slide deck for students to copy as a beginning template that includes information such as the answer and screenshot of search results.

Instructions

Step 1: Distribute slides.

Step 2: Help students share slides if they will be working as a team or with a partner.

Step 3: Review the scavenger items students are to collect. Show students how to properly cite the resources they use.

Variations

- Depending on the age or ability of your students, focus the scavenger hunt to a specific website or series of websites.

- Create a "Google Custom Search Engine" with specific websites for students to search. To access the Google Custom Search Engine and directions on creating the engine, visit cse.google.com/cse/create/new.

- Create a Google Form or other data-collecting survey and ask students to submit links to their resources in the form.

Key Points to Remember

- This game is all about learning search skills.

- Google "Google search terms" for a list of predetermined Boolean parameters.

- Learn and practice a few search terms at a time ("+" and "-" terms make a good start).

- To make searches slightly easier, include keywords in the question. In our question about George Washington, we included the keywords *Washington, rebellion, army,* and *glasses* for the search: Washington +rebellion +army +glasses.

- Include specific formats such as .ppt files, or other specific options in Google Advanced Search ("find a .ppt that . . . ")

- For seasoned searchers, students may uncover the needed words through a series of two or three rounds of information that build to help them to construct a better search.

- When searching on the internet for sources, always review the sources found for credibility and discuss how to differentiate credible from non-credible sources.

Consider the Following:

- URL location (.gov, .co, .org, .com)
- Identifiable source/author
- Cross sources
- Site design
- Writing style, including misspellings and tip-off phrases

When students find the information they are looking for, have them submit the website URL into a spreadsheet and then analyze the collective results as a class so that everyone might learn together about credible and non-credible information.

In-Between Students in Grades 2–3

The suggestions under the Adapting for Littles section (below) has some helpful tips for students in your age group. In this case, you will find these adaptations helpful.

Adapting for Littles

Searches at the primary (K–3) level will look very different from the searches of older students. Here are some tips and suggestions for adapting the scavenger hunt for them:

- Use a visually safe search like Kiddle.
- Build the search around answers that can be shown with an image:
  - Five images that begin with the sound of "t."
  - Six images that show a clock—write the time that is on the clock.
- Using an image search like Kiddle or the embedded search feature in your writing service, such as the Explore button in Google Docs, find three different images of a dog.
- Link a website into the doc for students to access a specific site and search for specific information within a website or two.

Hint: *Littles will need to be able to spell the word "dog" to be able to search for the word and then drag the image onto their slide.*

Chapter 22

Group Brainstorm EduProtocol

Have you ever asked kids to brainstorm ideas in class, and while three students eagerly toss out ideas, the rest just stare back? We find that many teachers avoid having students brainstorm since the concept of accepting all answers and even tossing out your own awkward ideas is a difficult concept for kids to grasp.

Description

Four students work side by side (or across the room) to generate ideas. Students will inevitably read the ideas of their peers and think of even more fantastic spinoff ideas! In this EduProtocol, all students will find a safe space to generate free-flowing ideas.

Prepare for the Activity

Step 1: Prepare a slide like the one shown on the right.

Step 2: Share it with groups of four students.

Instructions

Step 1: Define a brainstorming subject (e.g., Why do you think the colo-

Group Brainstorm			
Student 1	Student 2	Student 3	Student 4

Academic Goals

- Allow students to "play" off ideas while allowing all students to contribute at the same time.
- Allow weaker students, especially English-language learners, students with special needs, and shy students to have a scaffolded experience through the support of their peers.
- Generate many ideas quickly.

Teacher Big Ideas

- Use a quiet brainstorm session, which allows all students to participate equally.
- Create an environment where all ideas are accepted and considered.
- Support all learners.

nists were unhappy with Britain? Where should our class go on our spring field trip?).

Step 2: Set a timer.

Step 3: Allow students to silently brainstorm for the allotted time.

Step 4: Students comment on each other's items without discussing aloud.

Variation

Use the brainstorming activity with partners, using two boxes on a page instead of four.

Key Points to Remember

- Encourage fluency of idea sharing.
- Prohibit students brainstorming in isolation.
- Teach students to be accepting of everyone's ideas.

Adapting for Littles

- Allow just enough time for littles, who are slower writers than their older counterparts.
- Use a voice-to-text feature if available in your word processing program. Set to fourteen- or sixteen-point font so littles can begin to read the generated text.

When we introduce new tech skills to our students, we find that about a third already know it, a third pick it up right away, and a third have absolutely no idea where to begin—even after following a demonstration.

Even when we screen-record techniques as tutorials for students, a third of the students still can't figure it out and need a shoulder partner to walk them through. Getting around to help those students efficiently can be nerve wracking. Use the Tech Coach EduProtocol to allow students to be surrogate teachers for you.

Tip: Some like to call the coach the "conductor" or "navigator" and the novice the "engineer" or "driver."

Academic Goals

- Students practice techniques and skills with the support of a peer.
- Students learn how to help one another without taking over.
- Students experience receiving directions as well as giving them.

Teacher Big Ideas

- Practice with the whole class first, then partner up students.
- Let the students do the work.
- Don't overuse, as many skills will be learned simply by using the technology, especially with older students.

Description

Students coach each other on technical skills in documents or slides. They use a dedicated slide or document for evidence of their work together.

When showing students how to create slide transitions, pair a mastery student (the coach) with a novice student. The coach will, without touching the keyboard, help the novice through the steps. When completed, they trade places. The novice will now coach the mastery student through the steps. The mastery student should allow the novice to primarily direct the steps unless an error is made.

Prepare for the Activity

Step 1: Prepare blank slides or appropriate docs using one slide per student.

Step 2: Share with students.

Instructions

Step 1: Student A stands behind Student B. Student B completes a task, and Student A coaches.

Step 2: Trade places and repeat.

Variations

- If accountability of the coaching is desired, the slide deck, document, screenshot, or screencast—with the added tech element—may then be turned in to the teacher as evidence of the coaching. Or allow students to create a screencast of their coaching session to be turned in to the teacher.
- Use this technique for writing tasks or for completing math problems using electronic manipulatives in a slide or drawing programs, such as in the Google Drawing shown below; for example, the coach will help the partner group the ones and tens into the designated number and check that it was done correctly. (Two tens plus four ones equals twenty-four.)

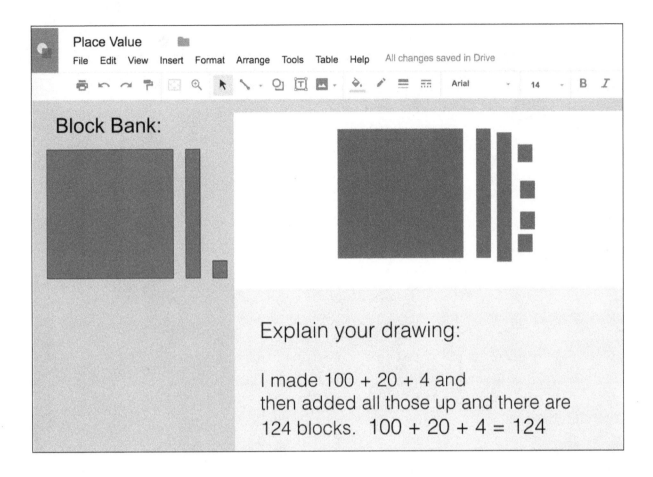

Key Points to Remember

- Start with simple tasks.
- Good peer coaching takes many reps.
- Once mastered, use them to support instruction.
- Model, model, model.

Adapting for Littles

- Use grade-level tasks and skills, such as adding images to a slide, matching words to pictures, or finding the answer to math problems.
- Use the technique for writing a complete sentence with capitals and periods or other grade-level skills.

Every year, in just about every school and grade level, we see students struggling with writing. Especially when trying to write interesting sentences and paragraphs. English-language learners struggle even more. And students are not motivated to write, either. Many see it as a chore. But we all know practice is the pathway to mastery, and once again, we find that short, concentrated bursts of energy with lots of reps is the key to success. The *8 p*ARTS* activity was designed to help students learn the "eight parts of speech" and to use that knowledge to generate paragraphs. Students complete the digital activity centered around the most outrageous images possible (appropriate for the given grade level) as the prompt. The funnier and crazier, the better!

Jon

8 p*ARTS is my main grammar EduProtocol for the first quarter or so. We do them daily, getting faster and better each time. Guess what the assessment is? Yup, build your own and do it correctly. Kind of like being a samurai who makes his own sword. Sentence p*ARTS is the follow-on activity that runs for the second quarter. With these two EduProtocols, I've established mastery, Four C's opportunities, and minimized my lesson planning and design overhead.

Description

Students work in pairs to complete the protocol, adding words for each type of the eight parts of speech to describe an image. They then write a paragraph independently, using the words from the protocol.

Todd Sinclair teaches sixth grade and shares his experience with 8 p*ARTS:

*I was really encouraged by what I saw my first year and was looking forward to using 8 p*ARTS from the first day of school the next year. I felt comfortable introducing it and running it with my students from day one the second year. The students love sharing their suggestions for the images, but many of them are shy when it*

Todd Sinclair
@sinclairt7

Following

Doing 8 pARTS and I think my class went nuts. If I remember correctly, the writing should stay on the page?? @jcorippo 2nd year is easier.

Students show enthusiasm for 8 p*ARTS, even when on paper. This student has extended the paper by taping on an additional page for his paragraph!

comes to sharing their paragraph. The paragraphs are messy when we start the year, as my focus is on the eight parts. As we progress, I start reading examples of paragraphs that the students have written. I don't give student names, and we review as a class what we liked about the examples that I share.

One of the first things students start to notice is that some paragraphs just use some of the necessary words, while others make a real effort to tell a coherent story. I singled out one of my students for praise. He hadn't been writing much with his paragraphs. He told me *he was always stressed about the space that he had on the paper. I challenged him to push himself to write more, and that if he needed extra space, he could solve that problem. The next day he had tripled the amount of writing in his paragraph and had stapled extra pages to his paper. I was proud that he took my challenge and just crushed it. Students asked him how he did it, and one of the things he said was that he added extra space to the bottom of the paragraph by adding paper to help remind himself that he can do more. The very next day I had students raising their hands to ask if they could add extra paper!*

*The students love to get a chance to share their word choices or stories. Students who don't feel comfortable with language arts will still jump in to share something from their 8 p*ARTS. It helps to build their self-confidence, and many of them continued to push themselves with the concepts that they don't feel as confident in sharing. They also look forward to seeing what crazy image I might throw at them!*

8 P*ARTS OF SPEECH

Adverbs	Verbs	Make a three-word phrase and label the subject and predicate			CLICK HERE FOR HELP	
					Nouns	Adjectives
		Write a short paragraph - use one of each part of speech.				
Interjections					Conjunctions	
Prepositions					Pronouns	
					Simile-Analogy	

Academic Goals

- Students learn the *eight parts* of speech.
- Students produce a paragraph quickly.
- Students work to increase their vocabulary skills in writing.

Teacher Big Ideas

- Shift work to the students.
- Students strive for mastery, not just completion.
- This assignment may break from the timed format in that if a student does not complete the *8 p*ARTS* Protocol, the protocol is returned the next time until it is done correctly.
- Complete *8 p*ARTS* individually to assess progress in learning the parts of speech.

Prepare for the Activity

Step 1: Create the template in a slide program or drawing program, such as Google Draw.

Step 2: Find unusual or crazy, fun images for the prompt. The crazier the better so students have plenty of descriptive language from which to draw.

Instructions

Step 1: Share the protocol with students.

Step 2: Students work in pairs or individually to complete their search for appropriate words to fit each part of speech based on the image. Pairs should agree on the chosen words and take turns finding and adding.

Step 3: Students write a three-word phrase.

Step 4: Students use their found words and the three-word phrase to write a paragraph describing the image.

Step 5: Use the same template over and over on a regular basis; just insert a new image for students who have completed their 8 p*ARTS to mastery (100 percent correct).

Step 6: As momentum toward mastery is gained, transition to independent work.

Key Points to Remember

- Here's the key to success: Utilize daily until around Halloween.
- This one protocol replaces dozens of worksheets in the first quarter and maximizes mastery.
- Follow with Sentence p*ARTS (Variation 1), which takes the class all the way through Thanksgiving.
- This creates reduced workload for teachers: two graphic organizers to model excellent grammar and writing skills to last about one-third of the year.

- "Grading" is done immediately as the teacher circulates the room and provides assistance as students work. Never take these home. Feedback is fast and furious.
- Go for mastery, not just "done"!
  - Return the same work to students next time if work is not 100 percent correct.
  - Allow classmates to move onto a new 8 p*ARTS when the work is completed correctly.
- As mastery is gained, reach for fluency and speed. (Lisa Nowakowski, a fifth-grade teacher, notes that her students will eventually be able to complete the math in eight minutes.)

Variations

- Use Sentence p*ARTS the same way as 8 p*ARTS of Speech. Be sure to use it after students have mastered 8 p*ARTS of Speech.
- Share your 8 p*ARTS with another class down the hall or in another school. Try sending to the same grade level or an older grade for individualized feedback. For primary students, this is a perfect opportunity for cross-grade buddies to interact.

Sentence PARTS

Imperative	
Declarative	
Interrogative	
Exclamation	Title the picture USE CAPS CORRECTLY:
Dialogue: Character 1:	
Dialogue: Character 2:	Use there and their correctly:
Dialogue: Character 1:	Use an appositive:
Dialogue: Character 2:	Write a sentence with a semicolon:
Plural possessive:	Write a compound sentence:
Singular possessive:	Write a complex sentence:

Adapting for Littles

- Simplify the activity. Start with just one or two fields for students to complete and work up. Have students brainstorm the word for each part of speech before adding it to the chart. For example, in groups of four, think of three or more verbs or action words for the image. Then write two down.

- As we scale up, we've included the interjections and conjunctions (below) simply because they are the most fun! Pronouns are fairly simple concepts, but first and second graders often confuse these: "him" and "her." Prepositions are simply position words and are also often confusing but within the grasp of elementary students.

LITTLE PARTS

	Write sentences using the words!	Nouns
		Person:
Verbs		*Place:*
walk		
		Thing:

LITTLE PARTS

		Write sentences using the words!	Nouns	
			Person	
			Place	
Verbs				
walk	drag		Thing	
Interjections			**Conjunctions**	
Hurry!			or	
Prepositions			**Pronouns**	
below			his	

Chapter 25

Math Reps EduProtocol

Fifth-grade teacher Lisa Nowakowski has adapted the 8 p*ARTS of Speech Protocol into a Math Reps Protocol. Using the same structure of 8 p*ARTS, students complete the math sequence centered around a concept or number.

Lisa shares her insights on the Math Reps Protocol:

In math, we often start with one idea (i.e., place value), then move on to another. In September, we work on place value. Then in November (second trimester), we work on fractions. In the third trimester, we work on geometry and the metric system. To me, this seemed disjointed. I noticed that students would forget skills from the beginning of the year. By creating a repetitive workmat, my students were able to continuously practice basic skills. Just like the 8 p*ARTS, the students were able to practice the same skills day after day, allowing them to master basic skills.

I alternate between the place value and multiplication/division paper. This came from a suggestion from my students and allowed them to continue to practice learned skills. It was a different process for me, as I asked the students to help create it. We came up with one sheet, but after trying it once, we wanted to change it. And we did. We looked at what worked and what we needed to practice and changed the sheet accordingly.

This should be done daily and assessed each week. The first week or two should be done as a group until the class understands what is expected. Once they "get the hang of it," all that's needed is the number, and then the students finish independently.

Note: A workmat is an editable electronic graphic organizer for students to work.

Constant repetition of skills has allowed my students to continue to practice previously learned skills and gain confidence in doing so. It takes us a while the first week or so, but in time, they will successfully complete it in eight minutes or less!

10 times greater
769,442.59

100 times greater
7,694,425.9

1,000 times greater
76,944,259

Add 10 times greater and 100 times greater
7,694,425.9   +769,442.59   8,463,868.49

Write a number that is GREATER (after decimal)
76,944.269

Expanded Notation (Form)
(7 x 10,000) + (6 x 1,000) + (9 x 100) + (4 x 10) + (4 x 1) + (2 x 1/10) + (5 x 1/100) + (9 x 1,000)

% (use # R of decimal)	Fraction (use # R of decimal)
.259 = 25.9%	.259 = 259/1000

Today's Number
76,944.259

Round to the nearest HUNDRED	Power of 10
76,900	769 x 10^2

Word Form
Seventy-six thousand, nine hundred forty-four and two hundred fifty-nine thousandths

Name ___Example_____

Student Number _____

1/10 less
76,944.259

1/100 less
7,694.4259

Subtract 1/10 less and 1/100 less
76,944.259   -7,694.4259   69,249.8331

Write a number that is LESS (after decimal)
76,944.249

Prime Factors of first 2 digits of the whole #
44 = 4 x 11   2 x 2 x 11

Prime Factors

Created by: Lisa Nowakowski @NowaTechie

- Today's Number—Have the student of the day decide on the day's number anywhere from billionth to thousandths place; however, the number must be at least to the tenths place.
- 10 times greater—Take the original number and make it ten times greater.
- 100 times greater—Take the original number and make it one hundred times greater.

- 1,000 times greater—Yup, take the original number and make it one thousand times greater.
- Add 10 times greater and 100 times greater—Add the numbers.
- Write a number that is *greater*—Have students change *only* a digit that is *after* the decimal.
- 1/10 times less—Take the original number and make it ten times less.
- 1/100 times less—Take the original number and make it one hundred times less.
- Subtract 1/10 and 1/100—Subtract the numbers.
- Write a number that is *less*—Have students change *only* a digit that is *after* the decimal.
- Prime factors of the first two digits of the whole number—Only take the numbers in the ones and tens place and find the prime factors.

Prepare for the Activity

Create the template in a slide, document, or drawing program.

Instructions

Step 1: Share the protocol with students.

Step 2: Students complete the template on their own.

Step 3: Use the same template over and over on a regular basis until mastery is reached.

Key Points to Remember

- Mastery of math concepts is the main focus of Math Reps.
- If work is not completed, return until done correctly and completely while allowing the remaining class members to move on to the next template with a new set of numbers.
- Make sure the whole class moves to a new template (with new skills) at the same time.

Adapting for Littles

- Use level-appropriate concepts and scaffold students until they are ready to work on their own.
- For first graders, the Number p*ARTS might look something like this: (We call this one "Number Time" for the littles.)

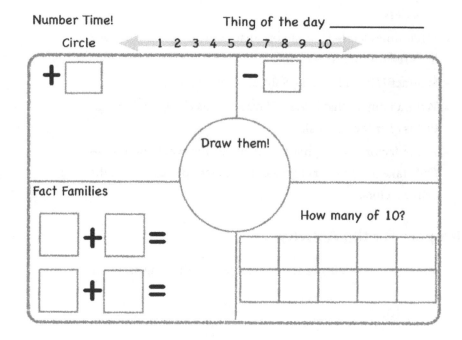

- The teacher designates, or "child of the day" chooses an item, such as apples, to be the thing of the day.
- Circle the number of the day.
- Then add and subtract 1 (or other designated number) and draw a sketch.
- Make fact families. (Add the subtraction facts for the fact family when students are ready.) Here's what you could list for the number of the day of 5: 2+3=5, 3+2=5.
- Draw the number of the day in the ten blocks on the lower right corner.

Shift the work from teacher to student and free up your time to provide feedback and support through the learning process by using the Iron Chef EduProtocol, in which students use a shared-template slide deck in a jigsaw format to learn content and practice presentations. Students will master the Iron Chef format best when this activity is used weekly. For the most success with Iron Chef, commit to using it all year long. You'll see maximum impact after at least ten or more rounds.

As in the TV show, *The Iron Chef*, this activity is structured to allow students to complete a task using limited resources and limited time. The teacher prepares a slide deck, to be shared among a group of four students, with links to content resources. The students research the content using the provided links and use the newly gained information to complete building out the slides.

Here's a note from Meghan Cannon, a third-grade teacher, about the Iron Chef Protocol:

I asked my kids today if they learned anything about termites from me during the past two days. They realized that all the learning was facilitated and done by them and they were really proud. I said, "I was just here in case someone got hurt, but you didn't need me at all." I don't have to work as hard, once they learn the protocol.

"You didn't need me at all."

Description

Time is of the essence in this activity. The time limit is what presents a challenge to the students and adds to the game structure of this activity. We have also found that students will fill more time with non-productive chatter, so less really is more! Students should be limited to a ten-minute build time. Keep the task simple enough to allow completion in the ten minutes, regardless of the grade level of the students. The slides will not be their best work at first, but over time, *with weekly practice*, students will gain the skills and confidence to build better and better slide decks.

Each slide also has a secret ingredient which engages the early finisher and contributes to teamwork in completing the entire slide deck. The secret ingredient is part of the overall score and might include areas of interest that are related to the main topic.

Secret ingredients may include the following:

- **Lists:** List five plantations in Louisiana and their crops.

- **Who is Who:** Who is Harriet Tubman, and why is she famous?

- **Trivia:** Which president freed the slaves on September 22, 1862, and what was the announcement called?

- **Facts:** List three facts about Lincoln.

Scoring is as follows:

- Ten points for technical accuracy (Are the facts and pictures good?)
- Ten points for artistic impression (Is the slide cool/pretty?)
- Ten points for overall perfection (speaking skills, addressing the audience, tone, and delivery—avoiding "Um, yeah" at the conclusion)
- Thirty points possible for the entire slide deck and presentation

Here's more from Meghan Cannon:

I have used Iron Chef for all subjects. What I really love is that only the reading level needs differentiation and not the activity or the content. I team-teach and work with two different groups of students for reading instruction. I haven't used the textbook in years, as there is so much rich online content. For my GATE group, I can use the websites directly, which is no work for me. My other group is slightly below grade level to very much below. I can rework the online content/reading into Google Drawings or Slides at their level, but they get to do the same activity.

Prepare for the Activity

Step 1: Prepare your Iron Chef activity of four slides and a title slide. Each slide is different yet follows a theme or topic of study.

Step 2: Link resources into the slides or in the note section below the side so they are readily available for student access.

Lewis and Clark

Your names here

Academic Goals

- Learn content using a semi-student-guided model.
- Work in teams.
- Practice presentation skills.

Teacher Big Ideas

- Be Ryan Seacrest: Sit back and let the students do the work and enjoy the process.
- Provide feedback to students in real time.
- Keep it fun. (We can't say that enough!)

Lewis and Clark

Click the video above or click
HERE.

Why was the expedition important?
How did Lewis and Clark travel?
What did Lewis and Clark accomplish?

Add an image here to
illustrate your main points.

Secret Sauce (to be done last)
See what it is like to travel with
Lewis and Clark. List some facts
here about the trip. Click HERE.

Geography

Visit this website and answer
these questions:
Click HERE.
And HERE.

What 5 Volcanos did Lewis and Clark see on their trip?
Why were these important?

Add an image here to
illustrate your main points.

Secret Sauce (to be done last)
See what it is like to travel with
Lewis and Clark. List some facts
here about the trip. Click HERE.

Sacagawea

Visit this website and answer
these questions: Click HERE.

Who is Sacagawea?
What was her role on the Lewis and Clark expedition?
What did she do?

Add an image here to
illustrate your main points.

Secret Sauce (to be done last)
See what it is like to travel with
Lewis and Clark. List some facts
here about the trip. Click HERE.

Animal Discoveries

Visit this website and answer these questions: Click HERE.

Add an image here to illustrate your main points.

What are some animals that Lewis and Clark discovered?
Why do you think these discoveries were important?
What could these animals be used for?

Secret Sauce (to be done last)
See what it is like to travel with Lewis and Clark. List some facts here about the trip. Click HERE.

Instructions

Step 1: Break students into groups of four.

Step 2: Each team captain opens their Iron Chef and shares it with the rest of their team. (Or use your learning-management system to share the slide deck with a group of four students.)

Step 3: Each student will edit one of the four slides for his or her team.

Step 4: Once everyone is set up and ready, set a timer for ten minutes. (Littles may need a little more time initially, but not much. Lower the cognitive load by keeping the activity simple enough that they can complete it in about ten minutes.)

Step 5: Students list five or more facts about the topic or question proposed on their slide, add an image, and complete the secret ingredient challenge. If time remains, they may then adjust slide layout and color. They may delete the information provided to make space for their own information.

Step 6: Students stop working when the timer rings.

Note: *Sometimes we see students add one picture and one sentence to a slide. That is not okay! Ideally, students need to put between five to seven facts on each slide, otherwise kids will quickly realize they only need four or five minutes to put out one sentence and one picture and will then spend the remaining five to seven minutes socializing.*

Step 7: Presentations! Each team has one to two minutes to present each slide, depending on the age and content to be covered. Just remember to keep the tempo moving.

Step 8: A panel of three or four "American Idol" judges are chosen to critique the slides. Be sure to name them after some of the original iconic judges from the music competition: Paula Abdul, Simon Cowell, Randy Jackson, Ellen DeGeneres, Jennifer Lopez, etc. These students sit up front, provide feedback to the team, and rotate after each presentation. You, the teacher, will play the role of Ryan Seacrest. Just roam the room, fill in missing information or correct misinformation, and manage the show.

Key Points to Remember

Use this protocol regularly to increase the tempo.

- Do Iron Chef at least once a week to build routine and capacity.

- Covering content quickly is a skill that students must master to be successful in school and beyond.

Build in scaffolding with video *and* text in varying degrees of difficulty.

- Kids will naturally navigate to the level they need most.

Front-load English-language learners and low or slow readers with reading material the day before.

- This allows students to participate at the same pace, or closer to, their peers.

- The reading can be reduced as well, or provide alternate, easier Lexile material.

- Video clips are an effective way to provide choice to students and allows students to view—rather than read—content.

- To maintain excitement and energy in the room, give students just enough time to build the slides, but not enough to get distracted with chatter. Know that the first one will be fairly poor, the second one will be less so, and the third and fourth ones will actually start to be good.

- Copying and pasting is always a concern as students become more tech savvy. Try to ask questions that cannot be easily copied. You'll find these at the higher levels of the Depth of Knowledge (DOK) chart.

- Don't focus on a super-perfect first attempt; instead, focus on a super-fast first attempt, which will get a lot better with practice.

- Stick to the allotted time!

Jon

Don't use Iron Chef to teach math; use it to teach math terms and vocabulary.

Things that can be Iron Chef-ed

- Presidents

- Key math terms (e.g., perimeter)

- Literary devices

- Science terms/concepts (e.g., evaporation)

- Portions of the periodic table

- Most common grammar errors

- Most common spelling errors

- Websites that contain content you can connect to the slide decks

Bonus: Try Iron Chef-ing with your peers. You can collaborate on your lesson plans for the week!

Note: *Iron Chef is not a good tool for large complicated ideas, such as the Civil War or WWII. Break down large concepts into smaller, well-defined portions.*

Grade Level	Group Size	Readability	Time	Links	Images
K-1	One deck for the class	Read material with students the day before so that the activity is not using cold-read materials.	Keep it simple enough so students finish in one sitting, as close to ten minutes as possible.	Start with one link in kindergarten and progress to two to three by third grade.	Provide images for drag and drop until students can navigate embedded search features on their own.
3	Two to three students in a group and scaffold to three to four by end of year				Image search
4-12	Four to six in a group	Use the same websites that will be used throughout the unit. Scaffold with different levels of reading material.	Ten minutes	Two to four links	Image search

Key Points to Remember

- Don't focus on a super-perfect first attempt; instead, focus on a super-fast first attempt, which will get a lot better with practice.
- Stick to the allotted time!
- Completion + Reps = Best Results

Adapting for Littles

- Use a class slide deck instead of groups. Review material ahead of time with students, especially material to be read by students so that reading, and reading comprehension, are not barriers to completing the activity. The task can be used with printed material such as a social studies or science book instead of online resources. And lastly, keep the task simple; for example, using the book, *If You Give a Mouse a Cookie,* by Laura Numeroff, phonics skills may be centered around the /ou/ and /oo/ sounds. Children use their practice readers to support their work in a series of slides which may begin like this:

Use the Explore Tool
to find pictures that rhyme with

Students search for words they find in their practice reader or from word cards.

- A primary phonics-based EduProtocol may look something like this:
- Students "hunt" for words in their practice readers and list them on the appropriate slide.

---

1. Read *My Creature Teacher*. Find **5 /_r/ blend** words.

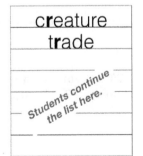

creature

trade

Students continue the list here.

Who is your favorite creature? Tell why.

Student 1

---

2. Read *My Creature Teacher*. Find **5 /_r/ blend** words.

creature

trade

Students continue the list here.

Who is your favorite creature? Tell why.

Student 2

3. Read *My Creature Teacher*. Find **5 words with ea**.

creature

trade

Students continue the list here.

Who is your favorite creature? Tell why.

Student 3

4. Read *My Creature Teacher*. Find **5 words with ea**.

creature

trade

Students continue the list here.

Who is your favorite creature? Tell why.

Student 4

From Meghan Cannon:

We've done Iron Chef with just pictures. There were slides for roots, stems, leaves, flowers, fruits, and seeds. Students just needed to find pics of parts of the plants that we eat and label the names. So even littles down in K–1 can do it with just pictures!

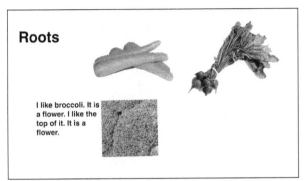

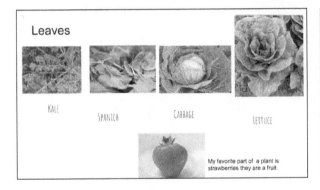

- Students would then present and explain their slides to the class or to their group.

Chapter 27

Primary-Source Document EduProtocol

The Iron Chef EduProtocol can be used in many learning situations. It is very versatile! We use it here to assist in the analysis of primary-source documents. According to Thinkfinity, sponsored by the Smithsonian National Museum of American History Kenneth E. Behring Center, students may analyze primary-source documents through different lenses. With some further modifications, we can apply the Iron Chef EduProtocol to a learning experience using primary-source documents.

Marlena

This variation of the Iron Chef Protocol uses expert groupings to deepen the learning and can be employed with any subject or grade level.

Description

This is an Iron Chef variation. Use the same procedure for this activity as you would for Iron Chef, except that students will work within their teams as well as outside their team in expert groups to complete and prepare to present their slides.

Prepare for the Activity

Step 1: Prepare an Iron Chef Protocol using primary-source documents as your source of information.

Step 2: Identify each slide with a specific Thinkfinity descriptor for analyzing primary-source documents.

1. Identify the author or source of the historical document or narrative and assess its credibility.

2. Appreciate historical perspectives.

3. Draw comparisons across eras and regions in order to define enduring issues.

4. Obtain historical data from a variety of sources.

5. Interrogate historical data.

6. Support interpretations with historical evidence.

Name of Document

Using the slides below (or the primary-source document) identify the author or source of the historical document or narrative and assess its credibility.

Insert image of primary source here.

Ask:
Who wrote it?
Is the source credible?
How do you know?
Are there other sources that might help you understand this one better?

Secret Ingredient: Find 4 interesting facts about your document.

Instructions

Step 1: Use the Iron Chef instructions for the Primary-Source Protocol with this one modification: Before students complete their slide, regroup the students in expert groupings; for example, all the students who will be completing slide number three ("draw comparisons across eras and regions") will meet to define, research, and draw conclusions based on their collective research. All students working on slide number four will do the same, etc.

Step 2: For this extra step, provide about seven to ten minutes of individual silent research time, then ten minutes for group discussions and comparisons.

Step 3: Expert grouping will work with any subject matter.

Return to the original groupings to complete the rest of the Iron Chef EduProtocol.

Note: *Not all protocols will use technology. A protocol may also be a paper-based, collaborative activity as in the 3-Act Math® EduProtocol and the Learning in the Round Protocol.*

3-Act Math® tasks are designed to make students curious about a concept through a video, demonstration, or image which is intended to leave a particular thought to be desired (more on this soon). Once the class has seen Act 1, the second act is getting to the crux of the problem at hand, with math serving as the vehicle toward a possible solution. Act 3 is the reveal, finishing the video, demonstration, or revealing the next part of the image to verify the work that has been done.

This chapter was contributed by John Stevens, author of *Table Talk Math*, coauthor of *The Classroom Chef*, and Instructional coach.

Here, John Stevens describes how he uses the 3-Act Math lesson in his teaching:

As with most new activities, we recommend trying a 3-Act task and taking time to reflect on the experience. When I first started using dynamic lessons in math class, I immediately wanted to do more, then quickly became overwhelmed, then stopped. I know, I know—and that's why I emphasize the need for reflection, which is easily overlooked. If all I'm doing is scouring the internet for awesome content and delivering it, the reality is that I'm not growing as a professional. While channeling content is okay at first, push yourself to reflect on why these ideas work, how you would change them, and what impact they have on your students.

Academic Goals

- Develop prioritization skills.
- Enhance problem-solving skills in mathematics.
- Make students curious around a common problem or idea.

Teacher Big Ideas

- Find a piece of media that has a good hook.
- Pause/edit the media at the point where the mathematics will help.
- Encourage student curiosity and exploration.

Once you understand the format of a 3-Act task, my recommendation to teachers is to aim for one per week, or three in a two-week span, eventually getting into a weekly rhythm. Doing tasks like these every day will overwhelm the students, so splitting them up is good for all parties.

The big thing I'm working to avoid is a one-and-done approach where I will try out a task, like it, then shelve the concept for the remainder of the year.

Prepare for the Activity

Step 1: Find the Right Video

Popularized by Dan Meyers, 3-Act Math® tasks are fun to do with students but can be intimidating to create by yourself. Fortunately, there are educators out there who have put together spreadsheets with 3-Act lessons you can use for free. Go to classroomchef.com/links and scroll down. You'll find plenty of lessons for almost any topic you need.

Step 2: Vet the Content

One massive mistake I made early in my teaching career was trusting the content I'd just obtained from another source. I downloaded a lesson that had a great title, matched exactly what I'd be teaching the next day, and assumed the author's work would be exactly what my students would need. Too often it wasn't. The video was not what I needed and didn't explain things in the way my students were used to hearing it. The lesson tanked.

Even though the people who created the content have a great reputation, what they present may not be *exactly* what you need for your kids, so make sure all materials are exactly what you need before going in!

Step 3: Give Yourself Time

Yes, 3-Act tasks will take longer than a traditional lecture, but the time spent is valuable and necessary for students to really understand a concept. If you are going to paint a house, you can go quickly, covering as much area as possible with as little paint as possible. But when you want to paint a picture to be framed for everyone to enjoy, you take your time. Find different ways to represent an idea, and let your creativity roam.

3-Act tasks will take more time, but the net gains in student curiosity are worth the extra minutes.

Key Points to Remember

- Be willing to take a risk.

- Let students get curious. (Avoid supplying them with the solution too soon.)

- Give ample time.

- Use the free lessons until you get comfortable with the format and start generating more ideas of your own.

- These lessons are designed to invite a struggle; let students struggle.

Adapting for Littles

- Some of the contributors to classroomchef.com/links are elementary teachers, so you can easily find tasks for whatever grade level you teach. After having numerous conversations with Graham Fletcher, it has become evident to me that every child at every level wants to explore curiosities that these tasks provide. In *The Classroom Chef*, Jamie Duncan shares a lesson she did with her first graders involving Oreos. The conversations that her students were having, the ideas they came up with, and the mathematics that naturally rose to the top were phenomenal.

- If you're going to create your own lessons for littles, you know your kids and how big of a risk they are willing to take. Once you've used others' content and feel comfortable with the model, we look forward to hearing about the tasks *you* have created.

Chapter 29

Learning in the Round EduProtocol

I(Marlena) stepped into a seventh-grade learning in the round classroom one day. Students were at the boards working math problems with partners. The teacher was circling the room, scanning the boards. "Good work, there." "Yes, that is correct." "Check your math, right here." Music was playing in the background, but what I noticed most were the smiles on the faces of the students. They were enjoying math! I leaned over to one student, and asked, "Do you like this teacher?" "Oh, yes!" she enthusiastically replied. This teacher was making learning fun by making math active and social. Two things middle schoolers love.

Description

In this protocol, students become the performers in the classroom and take an active role in understanding concepts by collaborating with their peers on whiteboard surfaces. The teacher stands at the center of the classroom and can easily check for understanding, provide reteaching, or ask guiding questions to large groups of students at a time.

The *Learning in the Round* format can be applied to a variety of subjects: ELA, science, history, and math in all grade levels.

Some of the inspiration for learning in the round came from Tim Bedley's Learning Gallery. For more information about getting kids up and working on whiteboards in the classroom, visit Tim's website at timbedley.com. Sean Kavanaugh was also a pioneer in learning using whiteboards to retool how math was taught

Academic Goals

- Make sense of problems and persevere in solving them.
- Construct viable arguments and critique the reasoning of others.
- Work collaboratively and individually.

Teacher Big Ideas

- Checking for understanding is easy because student work visibility is maximized.
- Persevere, communicate, collaborate, and ask more questions in a fun and low-risk learning environment.
- Share their thinking and different strategies because there is no "front of the room."

and was featured in the documentary *Teach*. More information can be found at 360degreemath.com.

Prepare for the Activity

Ed Campos Jr., former math and computer science teacher, now working with the Bootstrap program, describes how he prepares the Learning in the Round environment to get kids up and engaged:

Maximize the number of whiteboards placed around the classroom walls so every student can have their own individual workspace. Although students will work in pairs much of the time, it's important for each student to have a whiteboard section because they may need more think time to work problems out on their own before they share with a partner.

You can also start with an inexpensive alternative such as dry-erase sheets instead of permanent boards mounted on the walls. Some teachers tape off sections for each student workspace. In order to maximize the whiteboard space on the walls, it's important to adopt a minimalist attitude when it comes to the amount of clutter in the classroom and on the walls. Use a well-defined system to assign student pairs to work together. Some teachers use a deck of cards or a random name picker. As a bonus, add some music and music cues to the mix. Queue up a playlist that you can play in the background while students work.

Instructions

Put a rich, open task up on the projector and have students partner up to work together on the problem. Here are some great resources for rich, open, and visual math tasks: visualpatterns.org, youcubed.org, and openmiddle.com.

You can use a music cue to signal that it's time to get up and work on the whiteboards. I use "Get Up, Stand Up" by Bob Marley. Allow time for the students to collaborate and work through different strategies while the teacher stands in the middle or walks around closer to the walls and asks guiding questions. Use a laser pointer to highlight student work or address misconceptions and mistakes.

When you feel that most students have completed the task, have them stop working and look at their classmates' work to compare and contrast the thinking and strategies. I've done this by asking them to move two whiteboards to the left (while Beyoncé's "To the Left, to the Left" plays) to analyze that pair's work.

After some time, have them gallery-walk around the room to see the different approaches before arriving back at their workstation (I'll play Run-D.M.C's "Walk This Way" or The Bangles' "Walk like an Egyptian" during the gallery walk.)

Lastly, the teacher stands in the middle of the classroom while randomly calling on students to share out their answers and strategies.

Key Points to Remember

- Choosing a rich, open, and preferably visual task is key, especially in math.

- You can document student work with your cell phone or iPad and project examples on your whiteboard to discuss.

- It's crucial to allow students to see other student work via a gallery walk before sharing out their solutions.

- When students are sharing out strategies, it's important to highlight how several different strategies can arrive at the same answer.

- Switching up the partners often is key to creating a culture where your students expect to work with different people every day.

Adapting for Littles

Littles can use whiteboards in the classroom as well. Just get them up and engaged at the board. Start slowly. Follow pair sharing with a time for students to share out their process and thinking with the whole class.

Build writing skills with mini-reports by scaffolding writing through the year, and develop student capacity to write research reports.

In most classrooms, it takes students about four to six weeks to write a research paper, resulting in two to four reports per year. The mini-report is structured to provide students with a quicker turnaround (more reps) on the essential skills they will need for longer reports.

Jon

I got the idea from Rhonda Corippo as she explained the essence of report writing to our niece.

THE
MINI
REPORT

Once a week - all year long

Qrtr 1	Qrtr 2	Qrtr 3	Qrtr 4
Fact-finding	*Better fact-finding*	*Self-fact-finding*	*Independent, self-directed projects*
Fact-sorting	*Better fact-sorting*	*Self-fact-sorting*	
Note-taking	*Fast note-taking*	*Quality note-taking*	
Composing	*Composing - 3p*	*Non-chronological Composing - 5p*	
	Attribution	*Adv Attribution*	
		Source checking	

Academic Goals

- Learn to combine facts from more than one source into one report.
- Distinguish between relevant and non-relevant facts.
- Build capacity for longer and more detailed reports over the course of the year.

Teacher Big Ideas

- Model, model, model together on the board.
- This is a turn-and-burn writing assignment. If you take these home to grade, you're doing it incorrectly.
- Each mini-report is a "quick write" and is not to be revised or rewritten.
- Student growth will occur because of writing in the format *every* week. After about six reps, the skill increase will be noticeable. (The first three or four reps may be slow to develop, but keep at it!)

Description

Students will merge two complete versions of the same idea (two sources) into one plan for a one-page report. Start with three focus areas (depending on the grade level—building to six areas by the end of the year).

"Focus areas" are areas where the facts naturally clump together:

Presidents	Battles
Childhood	Location
Early Adult	Situation
Military History/Career	Opposing Leaders
Presidency	Outcome
Legacy	Legacy

Grading: At the early stage, focus on the task, not on the actual written product. The point of the mini-report in the first semester is to develop the skills needed to write the report, to find relevant facts, to interpret information, and to then merge information from two sources into one.

When "grading," look for the three most common errors made by the whole class, whatever they happen to be, and develop mini-lessons to eliminate those errors each week. Do not laboriously grade and mark up each paper. It saps your energy and does not produce student gains.

Use this criteria for grading:

- Everyone has a thesis?
- Everyone has five facts?
- Everyone has the focus areas?
- Everyone gets an A+!

	The Thesis or Controlling Main Idea		
Thesis			
	Chapters or Sections		
Focus Area	Focus Area or *Supporting* Idea	Focus Area or *Supporting* Idea	Focus Area or *Supporting* Idea
FIVE FACTS (not sentences)			

Prepare for the Activity

Step 1: Choose two sources centered around one topic.

Step 2: Prepare a Fact-Gathering sheet like the one above.

Instructions

Step 1: Students read the two sources and begin to collect facts and data on their Fact-Gathering sheet.

Step 2: The teacher, at the board, solicits facts from the students and writes them on the board.

Step 3: Discuss the merits of the facts and the relevancy to the report.

Step 4: Students add pertinent missing facts to their Fact-Gathering Sheet.

Step 5: Students write three paragraphs based on the three Focus Areas.

Step 6: Students cite their two sources using an online citation machine.

Marlena

I used a modified version of this Mini-Report EduProtocol with my sixth graders. It provided lots of reps and skill practice for my students and became a valuable piece of our writing practice.

Variations

1. Use a video for one of the sources.
2. Include primary-source documents as a source.

Mini -Report

Fact Gathering Sheet   Name_____

The Thesis or Controlling Main Idea

Chapter or Sections

| Focus Area or *Supporting* Idea | Focus Area or *Supporting* Idea | Focus Area or *Supporting* Idea |

Adapting for Littles

- For young students, there is no such thing as a quick write; all writing is labor intensive. Remember that reps build fluency and skill level. Keep the content simple and short enough so young students can finish and feel good about their accomplishments.

- Read two books about the same topic aloud (e.g., *I Am Washington* by Brad Meltzer and *A Picture Book of George Washington* by David A. Adler). Together, choose relevant facts concerning one Focus Area and record them on the board, then have students write individually, based on the collective facts.

- If students are ready for more and their writing development can support another round with the same material, return to the same books the following day. Reread and focus on a second Focus Area. Students will then add a second paragraph to their mini-report.

- For kindergarteners and emergent writers, after a shared readaloud and fact-finding session, each child folds a paper into thirds and draws a *quick draw* (stick figures) to illustrate three facts centered around one Focus Area. Encourage them to write a word or short sentence for each.

- Use an age-appropriate informational video as the source material and watch together.

- Young children can begin building the habit of citing sources by recording the page number information is taken from when using books as a source.

Marlena

This is different than beginning, middle, and end (BME) writing. In BME writing, students are focused on the sequence of events necessary for early comprehension. In the mini-report, students are focused on finding facts to support a key idea, which is essential to early writing.

It's what you do right now that makes a difference.

—Sgt. Jeff Struecker, *Black Hawk Down*

About a decade ago, I (Jon) came across an article written **by Cyril Parkinson in 1955 about how "work expands to fill the allotted time."** This declaration became known as Parkinson's Law.

In practical terms, if you ask your husband to vacuum the house by the time you get home, the project will begin when he hears you unlock the front door. When I bumped into that article, I immediately realized this law applied to my classroom in a significant way. Kids live in an alternate reality when it comes to deadlines. How many times have you heard teachers complain to each other, "I gave them *more than enough* time—why didn't they finish?"

That right there is . . . "The Suck."

When you tell children you're giving them plenty of time, their brain translates the instruction into, "I have plenty of time—why start now?"

How do we defeat The Suck?

The Recipe

I began to design a layer of work which allowed people to scaffold to the end of a project; for example, a recipe always tells you how long it will take to make. "This meal takes about two hours to prepare." In the kitchen, we can assume the cook is motivated to begin the work in a timely manner. But in the classroom, we must assume that kids don't actually *want* to do the work. Therefore, we must create a way for them to be comfortable doing the work and make the work as painless as possible. And one of the best ways to eliminate the pain of a project is to ensure that they finish.

Jon

If we do everything at the last minute, then everything could be done in a minute—right at the beginning. This is how I realized #panicNOW is an awesome way to get kids doing more reps, learning faster in smaller, completed chunks!

Marlena

One year, on the first day of sixth grade, I gave out math homework. Only three kids turned it in the next day. Apparently, The Suck can happen in less than twenty-four hours of day one!

Do kids receive low grades in your class because they *can't* do the work or because they *don't* do the work? What we hear from teachers is that the latter is almost always true.

Kids can get so far behind they become buried as the projects and homework snowball. They become truly unable to dig their way out on schedule.

The idea of The Suck is to face the fact that people will do what people will do, especially kids. When you accept the reality of Parkinson's Law, you'll try to structure around this element of human nature to maximize student learning.

Black Hawk Down

The name, *The Suck* kicked in for me (Jon) because I realized that Parkinson's Law was not going to be a super-attractive name for the kids to remember. At the time, I was reading the book *Black Hawk Down* by Mark Bowden. In one chapter the soldiers called their time abroad "The Suck" because they were going to lose that amount of time out of their personal lives, away from their homes, friends, and families. On deployment somewhere other than the United States, especially in wartime, they'd say, "I'm in 'The Suck.'"

So what does this look like in classroom?

During the year I was reading *Black Hawk Down,* I had a class of sophomores who were not big on writing. They were not going to finish an essay in a week, no matter what.

The old teacher logic is to give a week to write this essay: "Every evening, you'll sit down with your cup of tea *(Don't forget a shawl and a cat!)*, and contemplate your feelings as you write and rewrite this essay. Do this every night, and by Friday you'll have a piece that reflects your very best writing."

The reality was that this group of students wasn't going to do any of that. So one day, with about twenty-five minutes left in class, I said to them, "Hey guys, we're going to write an essay. Right now."

No way, Corippo. We don't have enough time! (I also happen to be an accomplished mind reader—or expression reader.)

"It's due in in twenty-five minutes. Do your best. Put your headphones on and . . . go!"

And they did. As a bonus, the students realized that by finishing *now,* they wouldn't have to worry about writing over the weekend. And they wouldn't have to worry about it every night, all week long. No one likes the nagging feeling of "Oh, man, I've got to do this thing." So why don't we work to eliminate it?

Marlena

I like my
cat. #JustSayin'

Learning to finish without stress

They didn't have that stress because they simply began writing. I also coached them while they were working. Because the students *completed* a project, instead of *thinking about* a project, they enjoyed a positive experience with the craft of writing and maybe even hated it a little less.

Former Mr. Corippo student on The Suck:

Through my schooling I often found myself in "The Suck." I left week-long assignments for the last possible moment and found myself stressing over work that was too late to accomplish. "The Suck" put me in an inevitable standstill, never starting the assignment until I began out of sheer terror of not passing the class. I frequently found that I had a

Marlena

This isn't about applying more pressure to go faster. It is about giving just the right amount of work for just the right amount of time. Instead of allowing the work to fill the space, as Parkinson's Law predicts, control the space to fit the work. And, as you probably already do, provide modifications for special-needs students so they, too, have the right amount of work for the right amount of time so everyone can finish simultaneously.

Marlena

Remember, just the right amount of time for the right amount of work. That's why, in the Smart Start chapter, we talk a lot about timing the activities, controlling the tempo, and teaching kids to finish. It keeps them focused and, in the long run, you'll be able to cover a lot more ground over the course of the year.

harder time focusing than others. It was never a question of capability, but rather a question of determination and work ethic. Since then, I have had to push through the discomfort and understand that being in or out of "The Suck" is a daily choice.

—Craig

We've all done this. If you say, "I'm going to give you thirty minutes to finish your spelling," students are probably not going to complete the task on time. But if you walk around the room and announce, "Five bonus points to everybody who finishes in the next twenty minutes!" you've just given yourself ten minutes back. You are the master of the time frame. Every assignment should have just enough time, but not too much.

Call to Action

Choose one EduProtocol and use it in your classroom. (Some easy ones to get started with are BookaKucha EduProtocol, Digital Class Book EduProtocol, or the Frayer EduProtocol.) Shorten up the timeline for the activity. Explain to students about The Suck and how you're going to save them some headaches. Ask them to buckle down and complete the activity before the end of the designated time. (Note: Be sure to run the EduProtocol the first two times with very light or fun content.) Repeat the one protocol you chose until it runs smoothly, using grade-appropriate content and sticking to the time frame. Remember to lessen the amount of content if students struggle to complete within the allotted time.

Painted into a corner, caught in a cul-de-sac, out on that final last-chance limb, life scrabbles around, searching for a new way out.

—Joseph Chilton Pearce

It's the day before school starts. New textbooks arrive in your classroom—boxes and boxes of them. You sigh. You want to be an innovative, creative teacher, but this new curriculum was chosen by your administrator, and you are expected to use it.

As you leaf through it, your heart sinks. You quickly discover it is a standard textbook with a fill-in-the-blank workbook.

But there is hope. The teacher's edition is a gold mine of instructions and resources. Contained within its pages is a wealth of content, big ideas, themes, and a road map to curriculum organization and standards alignment.

There are also vocabulary lists to support the content, and sometimes (if you're lucky) ideas for activities. You could sure use those.

The reality is that many teachers are not given leeway by districts to opt out of the adopted curriculum. Keep the teacher's edition on your desk and put the student edition on a bookshelf (along with the workbook). Student workbooks may stay on the shelves for most of the time, and student textbooks can be used along with technology or replaced with online sources.

Marlena

Notice that we didn't say "pacing guides." It isn't about being on the same page at the same time, it's about bringing depth to the classroom—and depth cannot be mass produced.

Lessons vs. EduProtocols

When moving from lesson to lesson, what's essentially happening is that we are going from desert oasis to desert oasis. Think about it this way: Teachers say, "Oh, I need textbooks, and I need worksheets. What will I do without them?"

The problem is that when you do the one lesson you found online or the unit your friend gave you on *The Outsiders*, it's a freestanding element. It's essentially an oasis in the middle of the desert, because all you have is some water and maybe a few figs. You can't live there for the rest of your life because there isn't enough substance! You eventually have to leave that oasis, even if you don't know where to find the next one! The transition is risky, and that's what makes teachers feel dependent on the textbook

There's comfort in knowing that there are 180 lessons, ready for the year, all in one book. And there's comfort in knowing that if you crawl from page 137 to page 138, you'll still make it through the desert by the end of the year.

The answer is protocols. If you decide to use Iron Chef once a week throughout the year, every Tuesday is planned. It's all set up if you move to a different grade level and ready if you move schools. You're still going to do Iron Chef on Tuesday. You can switch your subject from ancient Egypt to the French Revolution, but your protocol remains the same.

Using the Protocols with the Teacher's Edition

Let's look at how an innovative teacher can use the teacher's edition with the EduProtocols in this book to frame an activity and make it more engaging for students.

Jon

The other problem with "lessons" is that the students use a ton of cognitive energy on the task at the expense of the content. But the content is the meat. When we use EduProtocols, the task becomes second nature, freeing students to focus on the content.

Jon

Think of it this way: If you are a cook at a restaurant, would you need 365 breakfast recipes a year? I would argue that you do not need 365 different menu items. What you need are about ten signature breakfasts.

Example 1

Let's say the teacher edition suggests that students are to complete a typical textbook activity: Create a paper book, neatly folded so the pages are staggered to assist in note-taking during the reading of a unit on the four regions of the United States: Northeast, Midwest, South, and West.

Our first modification: Use an electronic slide deck for the notes as the materials are read or researched.

Or . . .

Maybe we could shift the workload a little more and try crowdsourcing the note-taking. Let's share the slide deck and take notes together in small groups or as a whole class.

Better yet . . .

We could use the Iron Chef EduProtocol to facilitate the crowdsourced note-taking in a jigsaw-type activity.

We could go one step further . . .

We could use the Frayer EduProtocol after the Iron Chef presentations to help students summarize and organize the big ideas.

Each modification allows for more Four C's potential as students collaborate, using critical thinking skills and creativity. The likelihood of communication in the form of publishing notes to the class, school, or web increases with the electronic version.

The content will stay the same.

The standards alignment will stay the same.

The scope and sequence will stay the same.

Here is how you might explain your new engaging activity to your site administrator.

In the original textbook lesson, students . . .

- Memorize (supposedly) vocabulary words
- Read
- Summarize content (critical thinking)
- Take notes

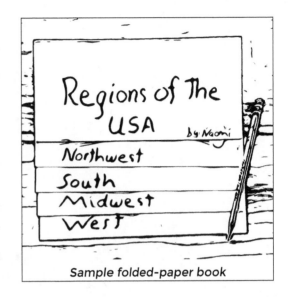

Sample folded-paper book

In our new, altered, activity, students . . .

- Read
- Understand vocabulary words in context due to immediate need (skill)
- Summarize (critical thinking) content
- Work with peers (collaboration) to create a slide (creativity)
- Record notes of the group (communication/keyboarding skill)
- Navigate web pages on the internet (critical thinking)
- Insert images and text into a presentation (skill)
- Create examples (critical thinking) to show understanding
- Publish notes to the class (communication)

All of the same content, scope and sequence, and standards alignment, but in an entirely new and engaging activity that embraces the Four Cs and allows students to be more deeply engaged.

Example 2

Students are to read the chapter and answer the five questions at the end of the section.

Our first modification: We could use the Frayer as a note-taking organizer. Use the questions as prompts on the Frayer.

You can also outsource the main ideas in the textbook and standards to online articles and sources. Use the Frayer along the way with the better questions you created. Come to think of it, we could digitize the Frayer.

We could then go one step further and have students transfer the information collected on the Frayer to a presentation. Then, using a modified Iron Chef, have other teams present the information.

Jon

Be wary of using the TE questions as is. They are, more often than not, lower-level questions focused on recall.

Marlena

But don't be afraid to use the TE questions as stems to help you write better questions. Be sure to use a Depth of Knowledge (DOK) chart or Bloom's Taxonomy to frame them.

The Protocols in Use

Now you can begin to see how the protocols, mixed and matched, can create a new workflow for students. Their proficiency with technology will grow, as will the students' ability to read and understand content in a format that more closely mirrors how adults process material in college, career, and everyday life. You can also see how EduProtocols are not one-use lesson plans. They are intended to be used over and over with new content—mixed, matched, and changed up each time.

So what *can* a textbook offer an educator striving for innovation in his or her teaching?

- Standards Alignment
- Scope and Sequence
- Teaching Guides/ Plans (to be used as a starting point)
- Vocabulary Words
- Reading Comprehension Questions
- Activities/ Extended Activities
- Video or Media Suggestions
- Electronic Content
- Digital Skill Games
- Tips

Standards Alignment

Most teacher editions offer a standards map so teachers can see where development falls within units and courses. Sometimes units can be taught in any order. Remember when you develop cross-curricular units, integrated curriculum often covers broader standards than single-subject units, including both literacy and content standards.

Scope and Sequence

There are many ideas and tools available for you to modify, adapt, or outsource. But aligning to district-agreed-upon standards maps can give a teacher-designed unit the clout it needs to pass scrutiny. Student work will provide the evidence and relevant documentation for a district that values moving kids sequentially from grade to grade through textbook alignment and allows teachers the freedom to design new protocols while supporting local initiatives.

Teaching Guides/Plans

I (Marlena) remember feeling totally out of ideas as a classroom teacher. I was tapped out. All my stuff was already on the table. *Just give me a book. I'm out of ideas!*

The following year, I was given a new ELA textbook and found that I regularly mined this book for ideas and modified the plans, looking for better engagement strategies for my students. The book, *To Be a Kid,* by Maya Ajmera and John D. Ivanko, which was the stem for Tommy's writing activity mentioned in Chapter 1, came from this textbook. I combined the writing activity and a project to form an entirely new activity. It was simple but much more engaging than the writing prompts and lessons in the textbook.

Sometimes we don't know what we don't know. A teacher's edition can be used to spark ideas. As you read through a unit, think to yourself, *how can I infuse technology into this topic? How can I use the EduProtocols in this book to teach this concept?* Skim through the ideas in this book and look for matches that can be modified with your content to achieve the goals of your grade level.

Vocabulary

The teacher's edition often does an excellent job of identifying key vocabulary and will target words that may be troublesome for kids. According to meta-research by Butler, Urrutia, Buenger, Gonzalez, Hunt, and Eisenhart, "Effective vocabulary instruction requires educators to intentionally provide many rich, robust opportunities for students to learn words, related concepts, and their meanings . . . vocabulary research confirms the benefits of explicit teaching over implicit teaching in promoting vocabulary development."

Even though your textbook will do a great job of identifying which words need the most focus, it is important to check that the words you use for vocabulary instruction are not words students will learn through the context of reading (Tier 1 words). Vocabulary practice should focus on words that are used across domains and domain-specific words (Tier 2 and Tier 3 words, respectively). Extend the efficiency of instructional time by focusing on Tier 2 and Tier 3 words.

Reading Comprehension Questions

Be wary of textbook questions and problems which tend to stay in the lower levels of Depth of Knowledge (DOK) and Bloom's Taxonomy. A few word changes can move up in levels, challenging deeper thought on the part of your students.

Be aware, however, that kids cheat when answering questions. We did. You may have. To avoid this, ask questions as a way to spur discussion or engage students in deeper Four Cs-type activities so students demonstrate their learning by applying skills rather than by answering questions. Embrace the community of learning and allow students to work together to understand vocabulary. (In other words, don't set them up to cheat—set them up to learn.)

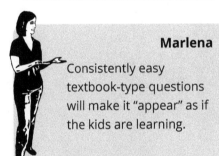

Marlena

Consistently easy textbook-type questions will make it "appear" as if the kids are learning.

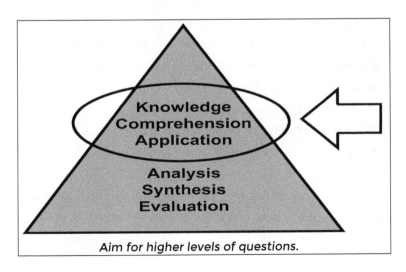

Aim for higher levels of questions.

Rewritten questions might be higher on Bloom's Taxonomy, but rote answers are not necessarily more productive for students. Ask yourself how else you can have students respond.

You can, for example, use your "new and improved" questions to help direct students to a deeper understanding of the content in an Iron Chef activity or in writing a class book about the topic.

Activities/Extended Activities

Define your lesson outcome, then use your teacher's edition like a library: Pull out what you can use and modify to help you meet your standard and curricular goals. Don't worry about the rest. If the content does not align with standards, feel free to toss it unless it is prerequisite material for later study. Look for technology-potential activities.

As a Resource

Keep textbooks handy as a helpful resource for younger students; for example, students may use textbooks to research a topic as an alternative to using online resources when appropriate grade-level resources are difficult to find. (Although it is getting easier to find resources at all reading levels.)

Textbooks pack in the required standards for *many* states and therefore contain more content than one classroom needs. The same book may have a California cover and a Texas cover, but the contents are the same. Publishers expect that teachers will pick and choose what to cover. But many teachers simply don't know how to narrow down the content and filter the most important from the least significant. Many teachers try to cram it all in no matter what. Not only can we skip excess activities, but perhaps we can skip whole chapters as well (and skip the guilt too).

Publishers are adept at marketing volumes of content implying that "Teacher knows best. We provide resources for options." So take this one step further and choose from the wide world of online and community resources in addition to selecting options from your textbook. One of Jon's friends said the TE was over-resourced, so he was under-functioning. Be picky.

In regard to Common Core Standards, teachers are finding there is a lot to cover in a year. Also, starting at about grade three, students must begin the shift from learning to read to reading to learn. This means if we proceed through the curriculum in a linear order, there is simply too much for a classroom to cover in a year.

There is a better way. We must use social studies, science, and other content areas as our text for reading as we begin to fold our subjects into one another.

It seems natural to read in social studies and to do math in science, but as we look at our core subjects, we see other similarities; for example, science is a story and sometimes reads more like social studies. There are plenty of math applications in social studies if we analyze historical data and trends. And art is everywhere. Art history can bring social studies to life as art is influenced by the events of the time (Art History Teaching Resources, AHTR). For younger students, American art is a fun springboard into content as well.

Marlena

It is exciting when reading takes off, and a student finally makes the transition from learning to read to reading to learn, but remember, they still need reading and decoding instruction through the grades! In fact, the K–12 literacy standards in Common Core provide guidance for teachers to continue literacy skills for all students K–12, in all subjects.

Integration seems so complicated. How do we do this?

If we start small, we will become masters at double-dipping the curriculum.

Start with standards. Familiarize yourself with them, especially the ELA literacy standards for your grade level, regardless of your subject matter expertise. We must all work to increase K–12 student literacy.

Next, review the content you will be teaching. Choose a unit. Do you need to select content in order? Whose order? Is there a pacing guide that dictates the order, or a benchmark to which you can align? You decide what makes sense. Sometimes content can be taught in a different order than presented in a textbook and be even more clear to your students.

Marlena

Think of it this way: the English teachers are not teaching students how to read history or science content, how to read a welding manual, or how to decipher a math problem. They might try, but you know how. Teachers of self-contained classrooms have been teaching content literacy for some time, but middle school and high school teachers are continuing to adjust to this new role.

Then analyze the textbook chapter for the big ideas. Make notes of themes. Look for places where the standards and the curriculum can cross within content and across content. Focus on one area and let go of the rest for the moment.

You are now ready to start using the EduProtocols.

As you fill the EduProtocol with content, plot the ELA and math standards. Then overlay the Four Cs to provide a multi-skill double-dipping approach to mastery.

Think outside the covers of the book. How might your students master the curriculum using non-traditional methods such as research, collaborative projects, expert speakers, or student-driven projects? Twitter makes a great resource for ideas, but you should also tap into your passions, the interests of your students, and the expertise of their families and communities.

Backfill with the textbook when needed. As your confidence grows, you will find that you will rarely need it. But when asked by parents and school administration how you are covering the standards, you will have the answer. When asked how you are covering the content, you will have that answer, too.

Most importantly, you are developing a learning experience that is deeper, integrated, and will more likely be remembered by students. Memorable lesson upon memorable lesson builds the scaffolding for future learnings.

As you return to planning the next unit, continue mining your teacher edition for information, resources, and big ideas. Then mix in the Four Cs and some resources from the big wide world.

Don't try to do all the work yourself. There is one of you and many kids in your classroom. Kids in your class are just waiting for a deeper learning experience—the opportunity to take hold of their learning in meaningful ways. Shift the workload and let students have some of the glory. There isn't a right or wrong way

Marlena

Don't be afraid to dream big, start from scratch, and backfill from your books. This might be more effective than remaking a standard textbook lesson into something it is not.

to begin designing learning experiences as long as you keep your student outcomes in view.

As teachers, we love to create cute, tidy little graphic organizers with lovely little borders for our students. We love having everything nice and organized into tubs, filing drawers, and on shelves. But life doesn't hand out organizers at graduation. Help your students learn to organize themselves! Repurpose your forty-minute prep period and shift the workload around.

The following is an example from the lower primary, but regardless of your grade level, it will help you see how the pieces can be put together to form a new reality for students.

Example: STEAM Activity and the Process of Development

What is the grade level? Grade 1

Which science standards?

NGSS Standards for Grade 1

1-ESS1-1. Use observations of the sun, moon, and stars to describe patterns that can be predicted.

What is our big idea from our textbook? Patterns can be predicted.

What STEM activity can we use to teach this science concept? Coding, using the Ozobot, a small one-inch robot that reads black, blue, red, and green lines by traveling over them and reacts with motion. Students can program the Ozobot by drawing the color-coded lines on paper.

What ELA standards can we tie into the unit? The following list was found in our state standards:

Common Core Reading Standards for Informational Text K–5

1. Ask and answer questions about key details in a text.
2. Identify the main topic and retell key details of a text.

3. Ask and answer questions to help determine or clarify the meaning of words and phrases in a text.

What tech tool can we use for this activity? A collaborative digital Frayer vocabulary activity! (But you already knew that, didn't you?)

Two students will create a set of four Frayer vocabulary cards using a drawing or slide presentation tool. We will use the suggested vocabulary words from the teacher's edition and make sure we cover the most difficult ones. We could also use an Iron Chef for this activity.

Now describe the activity that students will complete:

After watching a short video and reading a book with a partner about the solar system, students will complete two Frayer vocabulary cards in Google Drawing with a partner (collaboration). Then students will complete an Iron Chef activity with prompts, researched through their textbook and video (collaboration and communication). Students will then use markers to design (creativity) an Ozobot program on large chart paper to demonstrate (critical thinking) their understanding of the predictable patterns of a solar system. They will describe the patterns to an audience and explain how the Ozobot repeats the pattern (communication).

By reimagining the curriculum, we now have a hands-on STEAM activity, aligned to ELA and NGSS standards and the district-adopted textbook used with the Frayer and Iron Chef EduProtocols, which also incorporates technology and the Four C's.

No textbook was used in the deployment of this activity except a reading book which may have been a source of the science or ELA textbook materials. Most importantly, students engaged through the use of the Four Cs and the strategic use of technology, which moved students toward a deeper understanding of content.

Protocol to Protocol

Question: What's easier than following the prescribed text-book where each lesson is laid out with a matching graphic organizer, pre-made for students to fill in with information after they have completed the reading?

Answer: EduProtocols. Move your class through the curriculum, protocol to protocol.

You could, for example, dive into vocabulary using a Frayer every Monday in social studies. On Tuesday, research and write a quick-write using the Mini-Report EduProtocol on a high-interest topic related to the core reading or unit of study. On Wednesday, complete the Iron Chef EduProtocol or the related Primary-Source Document EduProtocol designed to cover the content and information students need. On Thursday, students present their slides to the class. On Friday, complete an assessment activity using an EduProtocol minus the collaboration, or another EduProtocol such as the Great American Race. A majority of the week's content accomplished—in four EduProtocols—*by students*.

Contrary to what you might expect, students will not easily get bored with protocols. They will find the changing curriculum keeps them moving, while familiarity with the activities is reassuring. Fill gaps with interesting student-generated, hands-on projects and other activities at a manageable pace. Before you know it, with four or five EduProtocols, a semester can be navigated. As confidence builds in yourself and your students, add additional EduProtocols to round out the students' repertoire of available activities.

Call to Action

Using your teacher's edition and student textbook, choose an EduProtocol and use your curriculum goals to complete one EduProtocol activity for your class. Consider The Great American Race, Cyber Sandwich, or Digital Class Book for your content. Plan and implement the EduProtocol.

Chapter 33

Mastery and Assessment

"If you tell me what Baron is planning then maybe I'll let you walk away from this." He frowned, "But I drove here."

—Tanith Low/Billy-Ray, *Skulduggery Pleasant: Playing with Fire*

Imagine you've just joined a beer-making club. You are so excited to finally be able to craft your own beer! At your first gathering, the brewmaster raises his glass and welcomes the group.

"Making beer is hard. Don't worry, we'll help you. But only about 16 percent of you will make beer worth drinking. A total of 68 percent will make beer, but let's be honest: Nobody will want to drink it. And the remaining 16 percent of you will, well, we have a packet you will complete to help you understand the process better. Are we ready? Let's go!"

Yeah. Let's go home, right now.

Some aspiring brewers will stick it out and try. Some will give up during the first meeting. Jon, for example, is super confident in his ability. He might even have some prior experience. He'll do great in this model. Marlena is not confident in her beer-making abilities. She can't tell a pilsner from a lager, so she might stick around for a while until she confirms her ineptitude.

Must we allow the accepted standard of 16 percent failure, 68 percent mediocre, 16 percent success, known as the bell curve, to dictate success?

If our car only started 16 percent of the time, we'd give it away.

If we successfully picked the kids up from daycare 16 percent of the time, we'd be in big trouble.

If Jon successfully barbecued tri-tip only 16 percent of the time, he'd never have dinner company!

We can do better than that for our students.

Ditch the bell curve. Let's teach for mastery, for the win!

How to Teach for the Win: Quality, Not Quantity

We discovered a marvelous thing as we transitioned students from paper to digital work: Digital work is so much easier to revise than work on paper! And our feedback to students became deeper and more consistent because it was also easier to give. Soon we began sending select assignments back to our students for revisions until done completely and correctly. Unlike paper assignments, electronic assignments never got lost in this process. We used to spend our time editing for the students, but over time, students used our feedback to revise and edit their own work.

We found that we did much less editing of their work and offered more guidance. ("Your subjects/verbs do not agree. Fix.") And students responded to that kind of help.

When students completed an assignment to their fullest potential, only then did we move them to the next one. Slowly we found that students were working on different versions of the same assignments at the same time. That was okay. They were all working, and everyone's work was getting better!

Now, this isn't the same as giving students unending time to complete their task. (The Suck!) We still taught them to finish by timing and collecting assignments, but for certain activities, some of the assignments were developed and revised by students until they achieved grade-level (or better) results.

The Old Way

Think of it like this:

Day One: Fifth grader Brett can write about two sentences in a fifteen-minute writing activity.

Jon

Here's a quote from my friend John Baxter (a learning wizard): "It takes four to six reps to move from 'know' to 'understand.'"

Day Two: Brett gets a brand-new assignment and writes two sentences.

Day Three: Brett gets a new assignment again and writes two sentences.

Three days in and he hasn't yet actually written a paragraph! No wonder it's fifth grade, and he still does not know how to write a paragraph.

A New Reality

Day One: Brett writes two sentences.

Day Two: Brett adds sentences three and four.

Day Three: Brett adds sentences five and six and maybe even seven.

He now has a paragraph!

Day Four Bonus: Brett revises his paragraph to make it more developed, based on feedback from his teacher or peers. That's a win!

Over time, he speeds up his process, and before we know it, he crafts a paragraph in two days, then a paragraph in one day. Now he knows how to write a paragraph! We know because he has now written four of them, and this is only the first month of school. Brett learned that he *can* write a paragraph, and he learned about the parts that make up a paragraph. He experienced the entire process and took the assignment to mastery.

Design for the Win

Pacing is tricky, and the dilemma is real. Not completing the grade-level curriculum will put students behind in the following grade or subject, but pacing too quickly can set some students up for failure. On the other hand, teachers feel pressure to keep the curriculum moving. In reality, the sacrifice of covering *everything* in the book is that some students will master *nothing*. Focus on

Marlena

We get it. We know it's a challenge to shift away from "I don't do that" to "Yes, I can!" Don't give up. Every class counts.

Marlena

Every kid is different, and as teachers we work with each and every one. It may still be a win if Brett continues to take multiple days to write a paragraph in month four of school. At least he is completing the whole process and learning that he can complete the assignment.

Jon

Choose your standards, then keep circling back to them until everyone passes. Growth is about breakthroughs, not incremental successes. You can't have a breakthrough in only two reps.

Marlena

I was sure that it was beyond them, so I was eager to move on to the next skill!

covering *skills* through standards alignment rather than the goal of finishing the entire book.

Students who mastered standards in the first cycle will go deeper. Those who haven't yet will have another opportunity.

Cycle Back for Mastery

We strive to organize curriculum for mastery. Cycling through the standards over the course of the year will help students develop skills. Students who mastered standards in the first cycle will go deeper. Those who haven't yet will have another opportunity. I (Marlena) cycled back through my curriculum over the course of the year to provide think time and grow time for my young students.

While teaching first grade, my school adopted a new math textbook. The book covered "ten more and ten less than any given number under one hundred" in the first week of school. This was unheard of, since conventional wisdom was that first graders could hardly write their numbers to one hundred in the first week of school. They usually waited until the last month of first grade to teach ten more and ten less. And even then, one-third of the class would not be able to do it.

While some of my peers bailed on the plan soon after starting, I decided to give the methodology a try for the whole year, even though I did not use the entire math program. I covered "ten more and ten less" in earnest, but by the end of the first unit, two-thirds of the class still needed massive scaffolding and modeling.

Mid-second trimester, they came back to "ten more and ten less!" By the end of this unit, about one-third of the class still needed modeling to complete the task. By the third time they circled back to those standards, all the students could identify a number "ten more and ten less" than another number. They were also applying "ten more and ten less" in solving addition and subtraction problems, abilities well beyond what my classes were able to do in prior years. Time allowed for the early-mastery students to practice again as the process moved into their long-term memory.

Rigor, scaffolds, and time allowed for the late-mastery students to grow into the skill.

> *Assessment of mastery does not have to be a test.*
> —Alice Keeler

Marlena

Easy differentiation for your class: Not everyone necessarily needs the same beginning slide deck.

Using EduProtocols as Assessment

EduProtocols like Iron Chef, Cyber Sandwich, Mini-Reports, and The Great American Race make beautiful evaluation tools.

1. Assess students using the same protocol that students use for curriculum delivery. Allow a single period for the protocol assessment and provide no assistance.
2. Create the task.
3. Set the criteria for grading.
4. Decide if the assessment will be "open book" or "closed book" and see what the kids can create on their own.
5. Allow older students to begin the task from blank slides.

Student Choice

You can easily flip your assessments once you have the format set to allow for student choice. Focus on what you want students to demonstrate and let them choose the means.

1. Allow students to choose their own media and methods appropriate to the task to demonstrate their knowledge.
2. Create the tasks.
3. Set the criteria for grading.
4. Allow the student to choose from a menu of two or three options, the protocol, and the tool for developing the protocol.

Jon

In the protocols-as-assessment model, the students work towards completing a protocol with no assistance. Once a teacher, school, or district has established various protocols as the assessment, kids come to the assessment ready to work. The only unknown is the exact subject matter. But they know the task. Too many times, we've seen districts have a totally different daily workflow than the assessment. When kids fail the assessment, teachers tend to make instruction easier. Avoid this death spiral.

Marlena

Do you really care how students show their knowledge if they learn and demonstrate mastery? Try providing guidelines and let them choose from a bank of options.

If using, for example, an assessment of California's History/ Social Studies standard for grade five, 5.7, you could explain the significance of the new Constitution of 1787, including the struggles over its ratification and the reasons for the addition of the Bill of Rights. One student may choose to create an Iron Chef while another wants to use The Great American Race with an answer key. A third of the class wishes to create a series of Frayers to explain the key concepts.

All of these activities can meet the curricular assessment goals.

Consider having students present their final task, allowing students another opportunity to speak in front of their peers. Remember to grade presentations in real time.

Examples of EduProtocol Assessments

Iron Chef Assessment

Using the Iron Chef EduProtocol, provide questions and links to information in the slide deck. For assessments, use information and websites that are familiar to the students. Or ultimately allow students to create and design their own Iron Chef activity

The Great American Race Assessment

The Great American Race is simply a collection of facts on slides. Allow students to research, or list from memory, facts about a particular event, concept, or question and create an answer key. To keep the activity away from rote memorization, provide standards-based curricular prompts for deeper thinking.

Cyber Sandwich Assessment

In Cyber Sandwich, students research together and then write independently. This makes an effective writing assessment because students have the scaffolding for the research part provided through their partner or group, but must eventually write on their own.

Other Assessment Tools

Use the following prompts to help students summarize their learning at the end of a unit of study.

Somebody Wanted But So Then Slide Deck

Somebody Wanted But So Then (SWBST), from *Responses to Literature: Grades K–8* by James M. Macon, has become a cult classic with teachers and students. The sentence stem is used to help students summarize a text. It is often used with nonfiction stories but also works well for social studies and history, particularly for students in grades K–6. Have students write it out first and then create a five-slide, image-based presentation based on the SWBST format.

- Somebody

- Wanted

- But

- So

- Then

Example:
- The King of England
  - *wanted* the colonists to buy tea only from England, and he wanted them to pay a tax on the tea,
  - *but* the colonists were tired of taxes without representation on the things they needed.
  - *So* Samuel Adams and the Sons of Liberty dressed up as Native Americans, boarded three ships, and threw the cargo of tea overboard.
  - *Then* the British closed the harbor to trade, and a year later, the American Revolution began.

Cause and Effect

Another summarizing technique that helps students connect cause and effect is as follows:

- This, then . . .
- This, then . . .
- This, then . . .

Example:

- The King of England taxed the colonists without representation.

  - Then . . . the colonists did not want to be taxed.
  - Samuel Adams and the Sons of Liberty dressed up like Native Americans, boarded three ships, and threw the cargo of tea overboard.
  - Then . . . the British closed the harbor.
  - The British kept taxing the colonists and tried to control them.
  - Then . . . in 1775, the American Revolution started.

Timeline

Using a slide deck is an effective method for creating a timeline and helps students place historical events into perspective. Students who need this context for understanding will find value in connecting events to dates.

Any of the EduProtocols will make good assessments. Just remember that students are demonstrating their skills and knowledge, and Assessment EduProtocols should be completed without teacher help.

Call to Action

For an assessment, use an EduProtocol that you are already using for instruction. Let students know ahead of time the general content they will need to study, just as with a regular assessment, but don't tell them the specific task they will be doing. Give the assessment and look over the results. Were you able to determine their understanding of the content? Did it provide evidence of their learning? Remember, you are not testing students on the protocol or assessment tool. This isn't a "gotcha!" Provide help with the format through the test if needed.

Chapter 34

Putting It All Together

Strong and content, I travel the open road.

—Walt Whitman, "Song of the Open Road"

We now know that a protocol (like a train carriage) remains the same, while the curriculum (like the cargo) changes for each trip. Link several different cars together, and soon you will have a functioning train. The different train cars are vital to the operation of the train, just as a curriculum unit has parts which are vital to student learning:

- The locomotive provides power.
- The carriage transports cargo.
- The caboose—the End of Train (EOT) device—monitors any damage that might occur during travel.

A train has a beginning, a middle, and an end. Sometimes you can move the cars around and still have a working train, but take out the engine, and it won't move. If you take out the caboose, the engine will be blind to the rest of the train and less effective in moving the train safely to its destination.

The crossing bars hold back cars and trucks that might keep a train from completing its route.

Most importantly, rain or shine, the train runs on a schedule, announcing its passing with a rhythmic whistle while possible interferences stop at the crossing gates to allow its passing.

EduProtocols

The Schedule

Set aside time on a regular basis so students learn the workflow. Start with one or two, and when mastered, add another until you grow your repertoire of protocols. We suggest that you repeat protocols each week to make them part of the students' routine. Learning the workflow allows the students to focus on creativity and content instead of technology.

The Engine

Choose your standards. The *current* standards provide the power, not the old standards, and not what you taught five years ago. Make sure to maintain fidelity to this criterion because the textbook won't necessarily do so.

The Tracks

Time and efficiency. The always-present, rhythmic click-clack. When students know the *path*, they can focus their critical thinking energy on figuring out the connections in the curriculum instead of the process of what they are supposed to do (i.e., fill out the one-hundredth new graphic organizer). Destinations may change, a track is not necessarily rigid, but the path has purpose and meaning.

The Carriages

You do not need 180 different lessons to make learning meaningful to students. Very few teachers can survive a year of teaching when planning a unique experience each day. There simply is not enough time or energy to last the year!

Build your repertoire of EduProtocols from this book as the carriage (i.e., container) for getting kids into content. Link them together and change the order to best suit the content and curricular goals. Add vocabulary in meaningful context and don't forget regular, interspersed student projects to enrich engagement.

The Caboose

The EduProtocol Assessment is another tool that can be used to collect feedback on student progress and provide valuable monitoring and data collection through the coursework, during (formative), and at

A student gains confidence in the engine of the train.

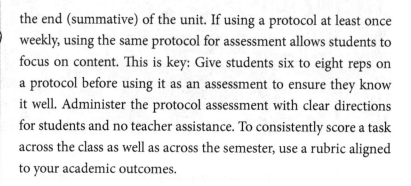

Jon

Make sure to start the year with simple versions of the EduProtocols and add details and subtasks as the kids get faster. Then the challenge keeps going up. That's a form of gamification.

the end (summative) of the unit. If using a protocol at least once weekly, using the same protocol for assessment allows students to focus on content. This is key: Give students six to eight reps on a protocol before using it as an assessment to ensure they know it well. Administer the protocol assessment with clear directions for students and no teacher assistance. To consistently score a task across the class as well as across the semester, use a rubric aligned to your academic outcomes.

The Crossing Bars

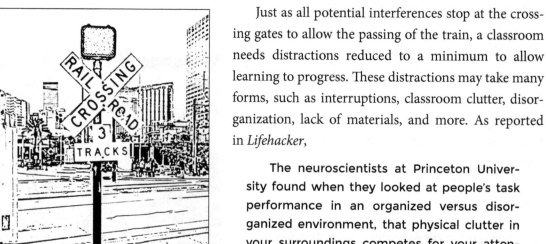

Just as all potential interferences stop at the crossing gates to allow the passing of the train, a classroom needs distractions reduced to a minimum to allow learning to progress. These distractions may take many forms, such as interruptions, classroom clutter, disorganization, lack of materials, and more. As reported in *Lifehacker*,

> The neuroscientists at Princeton University found when they looked at people's task performance in an organized versus disorganized environment, that physical clutter in your surroundings competes for your attention, resulting in decreased performance and increased stress.

Look around your room to identify potential distractions in your learning environment and work to minimize the ones within your control.

Not only is the clutter in a classroom a deterrent to learning, so is the clutter in our lessons. In *Nothing But Net: Creating Slam Dunk Lesson Plans*, Jamie McKenzie explains the idea of the Teflon lesson "to capture the idea of no stick and no burn. Directions are clear, simple, and easy to follow. Tasks are laid out in pathways that leave little room for error."

The Schedule

Conduct EduProtocols regularly. These are not one-and-done novelties. Student mastery of the technology and the EduProtocols will only occur through practice. A weekly schedule may look something like this chart. Remember: Students are using the EduProtocols to access curriculum, and curriculum is a daily business.

Marlena

Sitting in several student desks and viewing the room from the students' vantage point is often all it takes for me to fix the clutter problems in my classroom. Try putting a yard of fabric over a stack of boxes, or over a table with boxes underneath, to clean up the visual distractions. Or take home materials that are only used once a year. Walk through student procedures to see if they flow.

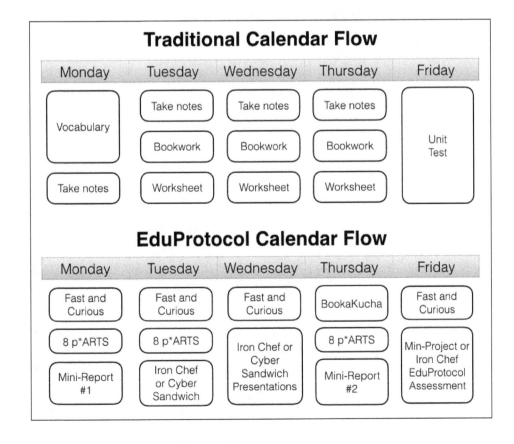

Traditional Calendar Flow

Monday	Tuesday	Wednesday	Thursday	Friday
Vocabulary	Take notes	Take notes	Take notes	Unit Test
	Bookwork	Bookwork	Bookwork	
Take notes	Worksheet	Worksheet	Worksheet	

EduProtocol Calendar Flow

Monday	Tuesday	Wednesday	Thursday	Friday
Fast and Curious	Fast and Curious	Fast and Curious	BookaKucha	Fast and Curious
8 p*ARTS	8 p*ARTS	Iron Chef or Cyber Sandwich Presentations	8 p*ARTS	Min-Project or Iron Chef EduProtocol Assessment
Mini-Report #1	Iron Chef or Cyber Sandwich		Mini-Report #2	

Marlena

Environmental clutter and lesson clutter influence the culture in your classroom.

All Together

Together, these elements make up the system of EduProtocols in the classroom. The train analogy can help us understand the purpose of using the EduProtocols for lesson delivery. Be careful to not confuse EduProtocols with one-and-done activities, games, or procedures in the classroom. Take the content as a whole, and use an EduProtocol to deliver it to students.

Call to Action

Map out your protocol routine as we have done here in the section on schedules. Envision the schedule you would like to work towards if you are just starting to use EduProtocols. Does your schedule have balance? Don't place all the EduProtocols on Fun Friday or Wacky Wednesday. Balance your week so that they become part of the fabric of the classroom. Also avoid "we spend all day Friday on assessments" mentality.

"I will take the Ring," he said, *"though I do not know the way."*

—Frodo, *The Fellowship of the Ring*

❝Look, this is my house!" a shy third grader informed me (Marlena) as I viewed the child's computer screen.

"Oh my," I replied with a grin, as I realized the photo couldn't possibly be of her home. "I think I'd like to spend summer vacation in your giant swimming pool!"

"How'd you get that picture?" her neighbor asks.

The newly confident third grader leaned over and began to teach her classmate, "Just go here, and then here, and then click here."

"That's not your house," another student interrupts. "You don't have a pool like that!"

It doesn't matter. Word has spread through the classroom, and now everyone is searching for their home, or attaching fantastic house pictures to the map pins in a mad bid to see who can find the biggest pool.

A few minutes later, the first little girl sneaks over to me and whispers, "That isn't really my house. I just liked it."

"I know," I nod with a knowing smile, "but it was *really* cool."

It isn't that kids are better at technology than adults or that they were born intuitively knowing how to make videos, or app smash, or navigate websites. They were not born with some secret knowledge that the rest of us are lacking. They have to learn how to use technology just like anyone else.

So what can we possibly learn from kids about getting better?

How Kids Get Better

Children learn from one another. If they see something cool, they want to copy and master it right away. Kids are persistent seekers of knowledge.

Kids are not afraid. They click right in and follow the leads presented with each new click. They try different kinds of clicks if one does not work right away, and they don't give up easily. When presented with a dead end, they attack again as if they are three points behind in the game of a lifetime.

Kids feed off the success of their peers. If one makes a discovery, he is the keeper of all knowledge—for about thirty seconds. His knowledge is quickly passed on in the form of enthusiastic help and confidence gained in the rush that comes with passing knowledge to others.

The Adult Version

So in adult terms, it might look something like this:

- Network
- Experiment
- Widely share

Network

We both use Twitter and Voxer as our platform for networking. Some teachers use Facebook, and others use Pinterest. It does not matter what an educator uses; the important part is to reach out to others outside of your own playground. Ask questions, be nosy, and share ideas. Most importantly, build a PLN so that when you get stuck, you have resources for assistance. Different platforms have different strengths:

Twitter

- It is incredible what you can say in just 280 characters
- Quick conversations with a wide variety of people you would not normally connect with through other platforms
- A great launch pad to meet others with similar interests and to then move to one of the other platforms

Voxer

- Records your voice
- Easy to listen to group conversations while cooking or driving
- Difficult to connect to people whom you do not know (You will need an invite unless you start a group on your own.)

Facebook

- A great platform for building a community, especially a public community

Pinterest

- Visual ideas
- Not so much a community in the sense that conversations do not happen as easily on this platform

Google+

- Another great platform for communities
- Quickly join a community in which you have—or would like to develop—an interest

Experiment

Try new things. If you fail, you can learn from your mistakes. (That's what we tell our students, isn't it?) On the day I (Marlena) first experimented in the classroom with Google Maps, I didn't know if the map could handle all twenty-five kids at once. It worked, and they had a fantastic time exploring and learning.

Widely Share!

My daughter was recently evaluated in her new job as an engineer, and part of her evaluation was an item called "Giving Back to the Community." In that section, her boss asked her what she was doing to give back to her professional community. This isn't something we have historically embraced as educators, but it's time. What are you doing to further your profession? What are you doing to help raise other teachers' abilities? Share. Share widely. It isn't too late to join the fun!

Some educators like to …

- Blog

- Share resources on Twitter, Pinterest, Voxer, or Facebook

- Write articles for educational publications

- Create a website with their curated and created materials

- Present at local or regional conferences and workshops

It's Not a Secret

Whatever you choose, tapping into the networks around you is sure to bring vitality to your game and help you be the best educator you can be!

We put our heads together and came up with the top five ways we get better at what we do:

Top Five Ways We Work at Getting Better: LEARN

1. **Listen**: Focus, ask, be curious
2. **Endeavor**: Make your own project-based learning
3. **Adventure**: Participate in Edcamps and conferences
4. **Read**: Articles and books (*Thanks for reading ours!*)
5. **Network**: We like Twitter, but any platform will do

Call to Action

Think about building a Professional Learning Network beyond your school. Choose one platform and get started. If you join Twitter, you can start by following Jon at @jcorippo and Marlena at @mhebern and begin building your PLN today! Join in the Twitter PLN conversations about EduProtocols by using the hashtag #EduProtocols. Follow the people you see posting there. If you already have a platform, reach out to someone new or join a chat group. A Google Site called "Education Chats" lists a vast number of Twitter chats and can help you find one that interests you.

Chapter 36

Because Cat Lady Isn't a Career

What is essential is invisible to the eye.

—Gene Wilder as the Fox, *The Little Prince (1974)*

Making fundamental changes in how we structure classes is not an easy task. Like a diet or a well-intentioned New Year's resolution, we know we must change our ways but often fall short. Then we restart with new intent, we get up, and we try again.

As teachers, we are so fortunate that our year and sometimes our class periods repeat. Over time, we are afforded thousands of opportunities to hone our craft. And with each iteration in our process and structure, we can get better.

Educational focus will change (we've seen three to four shifts in our careers so far), so we must constantly evaluate to make sure we refine the right craft. Are we refining platforms that increase creativity, playfulness, and curiosity in our students? Are we focused on crafts that help students for the long term to become better humans and contributing members of society? Are we using technology for the sake of technology, or using it to change our classroom—and even our school?

We worry about what will happen to some of our students.

A Different Way of Growing Up

Students in oversized red-striped jumpsuits stand out against long, gray, concrete halls. The cells are also concrete. Kids live there. Kids as young as sixth grade who were removed from their parents, friends, classmates, and teachers—and incarcerated. They meet new teachers and new friends, but at night, they march back to their cold, stark cells.

Few in the outside world want to think about these kids in jail. We didn't want to.

Yes, these children come from challenging backgrounds. Many have "complicated" home lives. Many have parents who worry about them. Some come from gang culture, but the bottom line is that kids were not meant to be in prison.

We've all seen them in our classes. We have all had that terrible hunch that a particular student would eventually end up there, or worse. We feel helpless in our ability to change their path.

What part can we, as educators, play in the lives of kids before they head in the wrong direction?

Consider the work your students complete in your classroom under your charge. Think about the most difficult kids, the shy kids, the kids on the outskirts of the classroom culture. Think about the Tommys in your classroom. Every child is full of life and hope and curiosity. We don't always know if we're making a difference for them, but our desire to do so is why we became educators.

Jon

John Stossel's "Are We Scaring Ourselves to Death?" references a study showing that, statistically speaking, the chances of being killed in a terrorist act, dying in a plane crash, or being murdered only takes days off our potential average lifespans. In contrast, poverty takes an average of five years off the average human life. When we educate the whole child and armor them with creativity, work ethic, and self-confidence, we are literally saving lives. Think about your profession in that light.

Looking Forward

Are we, as educators, working to refine the right craft so children can pursue their potential? It is not an easy task, but it isn't impossible.

- Begin with the culture in your class and leverage Smart Start to bring kids together.

- Capitalize on the big themes in your curriculum that develop community awareness and cultural sensitivity.

- Design engaging and relevant protocols grounded in Four Cs which allow kids to do the hard thinking and learning while developing creativity.

- Find joy in what you do and work to get better.

Remembering Why We Teach

As I (Marlena) sat in one of the last remaining seats in the church at Tommy's funeral with my head in my hands, I sobbed. I remembered Tommy, with his curly blond hair and curiosity for learning, running across the playground in pursuit of a butterfly. I saw his parents standing at the front of the church, remembering who Tommy was during his short time on this Earth. And the only lasting insight to his innermost thoughts and feelings at the age of five and six were the handwritten papers and art on display—the projects he had created in my class.

Our students' time with us should result in growth. Not just academic development, but growth as a soul in the journey of self-discovery. No one will display worksheets, black lines, and cut-and-paste art projects down the aisle of a church as a testament to a child's life. No parent is going to brag about the completed fourth-grade workbook. No child, alone in a dark cell, will reflect upon the personal growth they achieved on a worksheet.

Finishing the textbook will not inspire our youth to great things. But we can, in our classrooms, write different stories for our students, and over time, all these stories accumulate into one:

- Creating something that makes you proud and makes your parents proud

- Overcoming a huge obstacle in the development of a project

- Working with a tough classmate

- Developing a new ability you didn't have before

- Finding joy in giving and doing good for others

Identification and intervention for students at risk is a complicated process. We do not intend to detail a comprehensive solution here, only suggestions that might encourage teachers to begin to think about how to challenge students in a new light and to provide a supportive and engaging environment. We urge educators to seek assistance from school personnel for at-risk students.

Jon

We are the foot soldiers in a war against ignorance and loneliness.

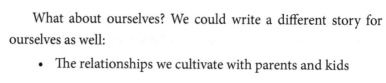

Marlena

I just pulled out my own children's box of school memories from under my bed and looked over the types of things that I saved. There were books, artwork, and stories. No worksheets!

What about ourselves? We could write a different story for ourselves as well:

- The relationships we cultivate with parents and kids
- Skills we help kids develop so they can succeed in life
- Instilling confidence
- Touching lives

Sometimes the task ahead feels nearly impossible. Some kids seem unreachable. Some present challenges that are outside of our ability to handle. Some kids drive us nuts with their creativity, while others circle the edge of the room looking for a way to complicate our day!

As Dave Burgess says in *Teach Like a PIRATE*, "It's not supposed to be easy—it's supposed to be worth it."

Preferably in joy, but sometimes in sorrow, will the artifacts of your class be among parents' cherished snippets of childhood past?

We hope so.

Will classroom memories of challenge, breakthrough, laughter, and growth be carried in a child's heart?

We hope so.

Call to Action

If you have kids, check under your bed and see what you've been collecting from your own children. If you don't have kids, check under your parent's bed and see what they saved of your school days. It might surprise you!

Next Steps for School Leaders

Smart Starts and EduProtocols can be fully implemented in any classroom while adhering to district goals and curriculum guidelines. And we hope teachers will see the value of using the EduProtocols as a way of effectively engaging students and delivering curriculum in a technology-based classroom. But if you are reading this book as a school leader, academic or technology coach, principal, or school administrator, we realize you may be looking for ways to implement EduProtocols on a larger, school-wide or district-wide scale.

As a school leader, your influence is tremendous. And quite possibly, the single greatest thing a leader can do to improve a school is to support the efforts and iterations, both successful and unsuccessful, of teachers in their quest to implement the EduProtocols.

One way school leaders can promote EduProtocols is to model them in the classroom and break down the barriers between teachers and implementation.

I (Jon) often join teachers in classrooms in the role of #EduGrandpa to model EduProtocols. It's the quickest way to help a teacher see the power of a new way of teaching—using their own students. I first ask for permission to do "something cool" with the class for about fifteen minutes, using easy and light workflows (low cognitive load) to share something like Iron Chef or Quizizz in a real classroom context. It is a lot of fun for the kids and provides a model for teachers to see how it might all work. Why #EduGrandpa? When the grandparents come to visit, they always enjoy spoiling the kids. It's fun and light with lots of smiles. An example of this concept is shown below.

Cori Orlando reflects on using a Classroom Handoff as a means of classroom demonstration:

One of the hardest parts about being out of the classroom is . . . being out of the classroom. Because of this, I try to find a way to get into classrooms as much as possible. I am very lucky that many of the teachers in my district allow me to come in and be "Edu Auntie" (Taken from Jon's #EduGrandpa) for a bit. Typically, these are planned visits where I get to take over the class and try new techniques or tools with other teachers' students. Sometimes they just happen, like when I visited Mrs. Wozniak's room.

Students were working in a piloted sixth-grade English Language Arts workbook. The students had just read two opposing articles about pit bulls. They were tasked with writing arguments (in a tiny little space) on whether pit bulls should be kept as pets. I know Mrs. Wozniak quite well, and I know that she was not thrilled with the task, but she was doing her due diligence in piloting the program.

"Hey, Josie, would you mind if I do something cool with your class for a bit?" Luckily she is a risk taker and said, "Go for it."

We used three protocols to cover the material that she was covering with the workbook. Afterward, Mrs. Wozniak and I reflected on the work that was done with her students.

Josephine Wozniak reflects on her visit with Cori:

Cori coming into my sixth-grade English class to change up my lesson was further proof that published curriculums do not always serve students best. While they create a way to address standards we have to teach, they do not necessarily create opportunities for the 4 Cs. We have to take what we are given—in this case a textbook—and design lessons for maximum engagement.

Now that Mrs. Wozniak has seen the EduProtocols working in her class with her students, she plans to continue using them with different subjects, ideas, and content. A win-win-win.

Another way to promote the use of EduProtocols is to use them during staff meetings. Look for EduProtocols that are appropriate to the situation. Here are some examples:

- Welcome back teacher or student handbook review: Iron Chef or Frayer

- Problem-solving schedules or conflicts with the staff: Group Brainstorm
- Making decisions: Group Brainstorm, modified Cyber Sandwich. (Compare and contrast can be modified to pros and cons.)

To replicate the Lesson-Sharing EduProtocol, with teachers, it is best to ask permission before stepping into a lesson and always honor the wishes of the teacher to maintain trust. (Trust is the most important part of working in the classroom with teachers!)

We recommend these tips for implementing EduProtocols school wide:

1. Start small.
2. Recruit willing and skilled teachers to lead the way.
3. Spread success from the early adopters to the rest of the staff via social media, staff bulletin, staff-meeting sharing, or other means. Remember to keep the focus on what kids are doing.
4. Build interest in using the EduProtocols with classroom lesson handoffs, model lessons, and staff-meeting experiences where teachers try the EduProtocols as students.
5. Begin with a simple EduProtocol such as BookaKucha. Teachers also love Iron Chef and the Amazing Race. Although they are slightly more complicated to run and require more prep ahead of time, they are well worth the effort.

Enjoy the process! You are on your way to a new way of teaching and learning!

Acknowledgments

We would like to thank Cori Orlando, Tammy Lind, Steven McGriff, David Culberhouse, Walt Hebern, Rushton Hurley and Rhonda Corippo for providing valuable feedback on the book.** We also would like to thank our amazing teacher/educator contributors for adding their voice to our book: Lisa Nowakowski, Cori Orlando, David Saunders, Trisha Sanchez, John Stevens, Matt Vaudrey, John Spencer, Ben Johnson, Todd Sinclair, Ed Campos, Meghan Cannon, and Steven McGriff. Thank you, also, to Alice Keeler for writing our foreword. You all rock!

Thanks to our spouses and families for allowing us the additional time we needed to complete a book: Marlena's husband, Walt, and Jon's wife, Rhonda, and children. You are wonderful!

Dave and Shelley Burgess, our publishers, have been amazing! And special thanks to Erin K. Casey and her team for helping us to produce a book that truly reflects the message we want to share. Thank you for working with us to make our vision a reality.

Mostly we are thankful to our readers, and we are excited about the possibilities before you. Your adventure is only beginning!

Happy teaching and learning,

Marlena and Jon

Bring EduProtocols
to Your District

EduProtocols Workshop

As teachers, how can we focus students on content instead of understanding the task? How can we give more feedback in class and spend less time grading after school? How can we move the Four Cs to the forefront of classroom instruction? In a fun, hands-on, high energy session, Jon and/or Marlena will share classroom-tested EduProtocols to enhance and reshape classroom learning experiences that will include tons of ideas to be implemented nearly immediately in a school or district. Jon and/or Marlena will customize this hands-on workshop to meet the needs of your school or district.

EduProtocols Keynote

In this fun and engaging keynote, Jon or Marlena will share a new mindset to reimagine classroom instruction through the use of EduProtocols to deliver content to students in fun, engaging, student-centered activities. UDL friendly and Four C rich, EduProtocols span the grades and content areas and students love them! Marlena or Jon will share some of their stories behind EduProtocols and teachers will leave with new ideas and tips for implementing EduProtocols in their classroom.

Chapter 2

1. Specktor, Brandon, "Word Power: How Artful Is Your Vocabulary?" *Reader's Digest*. rd.com/culture/word-power-art.

2. "Name That Thing: Weekly Challenge." *Merriam-Webster*. merriam-webster.com/word-games/name-that-thing.

3. "Computers and Technology," *Encyclopædia Britannica*, britannica.com/quiz/computers-and-technology.

4. Iron Chef is a registered trademark of Fuji Television Network, Inc.

Chapter 4

1. Spaghetti Challenge: A team-building challenge, introduced by Peter Skillman at TED, in which teams of four have eighteen minutes to build a freestanding tower using no more than twenty sticks of spaghetti, one yard of tape, one yard of string, and one marshmallow—which must be on top. For more information and directions, visit tomwujec.com.

Chapter 5

1. Photo by Marlena Hebern, modified in Imaengine

Chapter 6

1. "JOKE: Cat Vs. Dog—War of The Diaries." *Huffington Post*, huffingtonpost.com/entry/joke-cat-vs-dog----war-of_n_1534447.html.

Chapter 7

1. McMillan, Don. "Life after Death by PowerPoint." YouTube video, 3:59, November 5, 2015. youtube.com/watch?v=kRIcD7v-Vm8.

Chapter 9

1. Selak, Bill. "Things That Suck: An Epic #EdCamp Session," *Bill Selak Ed Tech All That Is EduAwesome*. March 15, 2012, billselak.com/2012/thingsthatsuck.

Chapter 10

1. Paper Airplane variation by Trisha Sanchez.

2. Image by Trisha Sanchez edited in Imaengine.

Chapter 12

1. **The Frayer** is one piece of a well-integrated and balanced literacy program. It was designed by Dorothy Frayer and her colleagues at the University of Wisconsin to provide a thorough understanding of new words. Students are asked to provide a definition of the word, facts, or characteristics of the word, examples, and non-examples. This graphic organizer will lead students to a deeper understanding of a word or a concept and its relationship to their own lives. "Frayer Model." West Virginia Department of Education, wvde.state.wv.us/strategybank/FrayerModel.html.

2. **A 20% Time Project** is when students use approximately 20 percent of their time working on a project of their choice, modeled after Google's 20% Time Projects for employees.

Chapter 13

1. "It's kind of fun to do the impossible." As quoted by Derek Walker, p. 10 Walker, Derek. Animated Architecture. Academy Editions, 1982.

2. Wallas, Graham, The Art of Thought, 1926. Reprint, (Kent, UK: Solis Press, 2014.)

3. Kim, Kyung Hee, "The Creativity Crisis: The Decrease in Creative Thinking Scores on the Torrance Tests of Creative Thinking," *Creativity Research Journal* 23, no. 4 (2011): 285-295. tandfonline.com/doi/full/10.1080/10400419.2011.627805?scroll=top&needAccess=true.

4. Land, George, "TEDxTucson George Land The Failure Of Success," *YouTube*, February 16, 2011, youtube.com/watch?time_continue=414&v=ZfKMq-rYtnc.

5. "The Future of Jobs Employment, Skills and Workforce Strategy for the Fourth Industrial Revolution," *World Economic Forum*, January 2016, www3.weforum.org/docs/WEF_Future_of_Jobs.pdf.

6. Pham, Sherisse, "China Wants to Build a $150 Billion AI Industry," *CNNMoney*, July 21, 2017, money.cnn.com/2017/07/21/technology/china-artificial-intelligence-future/index.html.

7. "2014 Otis Report on the Creative Economy," *Otis College of Art and Design*, April 2015, otis.edu/sites/default/files/2015_Otis_Report_on_the_Creative_Economy_CA.pdf.

8. Guerrini, Federico, "The Future of Agriculture? Smart Farming," *Forbes*, Forbes Magazine, September 19, 2015, forbes.com/sites/federicoguerrini/2015/02/18/the-future-of-agriculture-smart-farming/#120600753c42.

9. Mazur, Michal. "Six Ways Drones Are Revolutionizing Agriculture." *MIT Technology Review*, July 22, 2016. technologyreview.com/s/601935/six-ways-drones-are-revolutionizing-agriculture.

10. Romero, Dennis. "Entertainment Leads a Creative Economy Worth $293.8 Billion to California." *LA Weekly*, Apr. 16, 2015. laweekly.com/news/entertainment-leads-a-creative-economy-worth-2938-billion-to-california-5499506.

11. Walker, Derek, *Animated Architecture (Architectural Design Profile)*, Academy Editions Ltd, December 1982, 10.

12. "State Schools Chief Tom Torlakson Supports New Legislation to Promote Media Arts in Education." *California Department of Education*, December 5, 2016, cde.ca.gov/nr/ne/yr16/yr16rel81.asp.

13. "Fast Facts on California's Innovation Economy," *California State Assembly*, ajed.assembly.ca.gov/keyinsightsintoinnovation.

Chapter 14

1. Wagner, Tony, *The Global Achievement Gap: Why Even Our Best Schools Don't Teach the New Survival Skills Our Children Need—and What We Can Do About It* (New York, NY: Basic Books, 2008).

2. Popova, Maria. "Philosopher Erich Fromm on the Art of Loving and What Is Keeping Us from Mastering It." *Brain Pickings*. brainpickings.org/2015/10/29/the-art-of-loving-erich-fromm/.

3. Four Cs Image: Kahoot.com.

4. Klingensmith, Bob, "History-social Science Content Standards for California Public Schools: Kindergarten through Grade Twelve." California State Board of Education, cde.ca.gov/be/st/ss/.

5. Boyd, Chase, "Literary Devices in Song," *vimeo*, 2012.

6. Stevens, John and Vaudrey, Matt, *The Classroom Chef: Sharpen Your Lessons, Season Your Classes, Make Math Meaningful*, (San Diego, CA: Dave Burgess Consulting, 2016) 75-80.

Chapter 15

1. Marzano, Robert, "The Roberto Marzano's 9 Effective Instructional Strategies Infographic." *E-Learning Infographics*. elearninginfographics.com/the-roberto-marzanos-9-effective-instructional-strategies-infographic/.

2. Cooperative vs. Collaborative Image by John Spencer @spencerideas spencerauthor.com.

3. Presentation Slides vs. Report Slides: Images by Marlena Hebern.

Chapter 16

1. Frayer, Dorothy, "A Schema for Testing the Level of Concept Mastery," Working Paper. Madison, WI: n.p., 1969, PDF, brainimaging. waisman.wisc.edu/~perlman/frayer-frederick-klausmeier.pdf.

Chapter 17

1. BookaKucha EduProtocol by Marlena Hebern (and named by Jon).

Chapter 19

1. Great American Race EduProtocol by Ben Johnson.

2. Motown Image: Walt Hebern.

3. Heidelberg Project Image: Marlena Hebern.

4. Michigan State Capitol Image: Marlena Hebern.

5. "Facts About Michigan Agriculture," *Department of Agriculture and Rural Development (MDARD)*, michigan.gov/mda rd/0,4610,7-125-1572-7775--,00.html.

6. "List of U.S. State Birds," *Wikipedia*, en.wikipedia.org/wiki/List_of_U.S._state_birds.

7. The Amazing Race Variation: Created by David Saunders.

Chapter 20

1. Cyber Sandwich by Marlena Hebern.

2. Marzano, Robert, Debra Pickering, and Jane Pollock, "Nine Essential Instructional Strategies," from *Classroom Instruction that Works: Research-Based Strategies for Increasing Student Achievement,* (ASCD: Alexandria, Virginia, 2001).

3. Photo by Marlena Hebern, modified in Imaengine.

Chapter 21

1. Zeus Image by Julie, edited in Imaengine.

Chapter 22

1. Group Brainstorm Protocol by Marlena Hebern.

Chapter 23

1. Tech Coach EduProtocol by Marlena Hebern.

Chapter 24

1. 8 p*ARTS Protocol by Jon Corippo.

2. Sinclair, Todd. Twitter post.

Chapter 25

1. Variation: Math Parts adapted and written by Lisa Nowakowski.

Chapter 26

1. Iron Chef EduProtocol by Jon Corippo.

2. Students Iron Chef-ing Image: Meghan Cannon and modified in Imaengine.

3. Vegetable Iron Chef: Student work (student names have been changed) from Meghan Cannon's third-grade class. Original images have been replaced with similar images from Pixabay.

4. Cat Iron Chef Image: Pixabay.

Chapter 27

1. Primary-Source Protocol by Marlena Hebern.

2. "Engaging Students with Primary Sources," *Thinkfinity*, historyexplorer.si.edu/sites/default/files/PrimarySources.pdf.

3. Rael, Patrick, "How to Read a Primary Source," The University of Iowa College of Liberal Arts and Sciences, clas.uiowa.edu/history/teaching-and-writing-center/guides/source-identification/primary-source.

Chapter 28

1. 3-Act Math® Lesson: Dan Meyers.

Chapter 29

1. "Standards for Mathematical Practice." *Common Core State Standards Initiative,* corestandards.org/Math/Practice.

2. Liljedahl, Peter, *Posing and Solving Mathematical Problems,* Cham Springer, 1986, springer.com/us/book/9783319280219?wt_mc=ThirdParty.SpringerLink.3.EPR653.About_eBook.

3. Kavanaugh Sean, "360 Degree Math," 360degreemath.com.

4. Bedley, Tim. "Gallery Learning," *Tim Bedley. Elementary Education and More* (blog), timbedley.com.

5. Dry erase sheets: Amazon bit.ly/GoWrite25.

6. Images by Ed Campos, edited in Imaengine.

Chapter 30

1. Mini-Report Protocol, originally developed by Rhonda Corippo, modified by Jon Corippo and later re-modified by Marlena Hebern (How's that for iterations?).

Chapter 31

1. Parkinson, Cyril Northcote, "Parkinson's Law," *The Economist Archives,* economist.com/node/14116121.

2. Bowden, Mark, *Black Hawk Down: A Story of Modern War.* (New York, NY: Grove Press, 1999).

Chapter 32

1. Butler, Shari, Kelsi Urrutia, Anneta Buenger, Nina Gonzalez, Marla Hunt, and Corinne Eisenhart, "A Review of the Current Research on Vocabulary Instruction," *National Reading Technical Assistance Center,* ed.gov/programs/readingfirst/support/rmcfinal1.pdf.

2. Koehler, Karen, "Art and Political Commitment." *Art History Teaching Resources,* arthistoryteachingresources.org/lessons/art-and-political-commitment/.

3. "On Creating Art in Times of Political Unrest." *New Yorker* video. video.newyorker.com/watch/on-creating-art-in-times-of-political-unrest.

4. "English/Language Arts Content Standards for California Public Schools," *California State Board of Education,* cde.ca.gov/be/st/ss/documents/elacontentstnds.pdf.

5. "NGSS Standards," *California Department of Education,* cde.ca.gov/pd/ca/sc/documents/cangss-gr1-topic-mar2015.doc.

Chapter 33

1. Klingensmith, Bob, "History-social Science Content Standards for California Public Schools: Kindergarten through Grade Twelve." California State Board of Education, cde.ca.gov/be/st/ss/.

2. Macon, James M, *Responses to Literature: Grades K-8,* (Newark, DE: *International Reading Association,* 1991).

3. Image by Jon Corippo, edited in Imaengine.

Chapter 34

1. Image: Train engine by Pixabay, modified in Imaengine.

2. Images: California State Railroad Museum trains and boy in engine by Marlena Hebern, modified in Imaengine.

3. McKenzie, Jamie. "Nothing but Net: Creating Slam Dunk Lesson Plans." *EdTech Focus on K-12,* March/April 2006. edtechmagazine.com/k12/article/2006/10/how-create-slam-dunk-digital-lessons-sdls.

Chapter 36

1. Photo: Graduation of Elaina by Marlena Hebern, modified in Imaengine.

2. Photo: Chain link fence, Pixabay, modified in Imaengine.

3. Photo: Class by Jon Corippo, modified in Imaengine.

4. No cats or cat ladies were harmed in the making of this book; in fact, we love them both!!

More from

DAVE BURGESS Consulting, Inc.

Teach Like a PIRATE
Increase Student Engagement, Boost Your Creativity, and Transform Your Life as an Educator

By Dave Burgess (@BurgessDave)

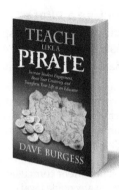

Teach Like a PIRATE is the *New York Times'* best-selling book that has sparked a worldwide educational revolution. It is part inspirational manifesto that ignites passion for the profession and part practical road map, filled with dynamic strategies to dramatically increase student engagement. Translated into multiple languages, its message resonates with educators who want to design outrageously creative lessons and transform school into a life-changing experience for students.

Learn Like a PIRATE
Empower Your Students to Collaborate, Lead, and Succeed

By Paul Solarz (@PaulSolarz)

Today's job market demands that students be prepared to take responsibility for their lives and careers. We do them a disservice if we teach them how to earn passing grades without equipping them to take charge of their education. In *Learn Like a PIRATE*, Paul Solarz explains how to design classroom experiences that encourage students to take risks and explore their passions in a stimulating, motivating, and supportive environment where improvement, rather than grades, is the focus. Discover how student-led classrooms help students thrive and develop into self-directed, confident citizens who are capable of making smart, responsible decisions, all on their own.

P is for PIRATE
Inspirational ABC's for Educators

By Dave and Shelley Burgess (@Burgess_Shelley)

Teaching is an adventure that stretches the imagination and calls for creativity every day! In *P is for PIRATE*, husband and wife team Dave and Shelley Burgess encourage and inspire educators to make their classrooms fun and exciting places to learn. Tapping into years of personal experience and drawing on the insights of more than seventy educators, the authors offer a wealth of ideas for making learning and teaching more fulfilling than ever before.

Play Like a Pirate

Engage Students with Toys, Games, and Comics. Make Your Classroom Fun Again!

By Quinn Rollins (@jedikermit)

Yes! School can be simultaneously fun and educational. In *Play Like a Pirate*, Quinn Rollins offers practical, engaging strategies and resources that make it easy to integrate fun into your curriculum. Regardless of the grade level you teach, you'll find inspiration and ideas that will help you engage your students in unforgettable ways.

eXPlore Like a Pirate

Gamification and Game-Inspired Course Design to Engage, Enrich, and Elevate Your Learners

By Michael Matera (@MrMatera)

Are you ready to transform your classroom into an experiential world that flourishes on collaboration and creativity? Then set sail with classroom game designer and educator Michael Matera as he reveals the possibilities and power of game-based learning. In *eXPlore Like a Pirate*, Matera serves as your experienced guide to help you apply the most motivational techniques of gameplay to your classroom. You'll learn gamification strategies that will work with and enhance (rather than replace) your current curriculum and discover how these engaging methods can be applied to any grade level or subject.

The Innovator's Mindset

Empower Learning, Unleash Talent, and Lead a Culture of Creativity

By George Couros (@gcouros)

The traditional system of education requires students to hold their questions and compliantly stick to the scheduled curriculum. But our job as educators is to provide new and better opportunities for our students. It's time to recognize that compliance doesn't foster innovation, encourage critical thinking, or inspire creativity—and those are the skills our students need to succeed. In *The Innovator's Mindset*, George Couros encourages teachers and administrators to empower their learners to wonder, to explore—and to become forward-thinking leaders.

Master the Media

How Teaching Media Literacy Can Save Our Plugged-in World

By Julie Smith (@julnilsmith)

Written to help teachers and parents educate the next generation, *Master the Media* explains the history, purpose, and messages behind the media. The point isn't to get kids to unplug; it's to help them make informed choices, understand the difference between truth and lies, and discern perception from reality. Critical thinking leads to smarter decisions—and it's why media literacy can save the world.

The Zen Teacher
Creating FOCUS, SIMPLICITY, and TRANQUILITY in the Classroom
By Dan Tricarico (@TheZenTeacher)

Teachers have incredible power to influence—even improve—the future. In *The Zen Teacher*, educator, blogger, and speaker Dan Tricarico provides practical, easy-to-use techniques to help teachers be their best—unrushed and fully focused—so they can maximize their performance and improve their quality of life. In this introductory guide, Dan Tricarico explains what it means to develop a Zen practice—something that has nothing to do with religion and everything to do with your ability to thrive in the classroom.

Lead Like a PIRATE
Make School Amazing for Your Students and Staff
By Shelley Burgess and Beth Houf (@Burgess_Shelley, @BethHouf)

In Lead Like a PIRATE, education leaders Shelley Burgess and Beth Houf map out the character traits necessary to captain a school or district. You'll learn where to find the treasure that's already in your classrooms and schools—and how to bring out the very best in your educators. This book will equip and encourage you to be relentless in your quest to make school amazing for your students, staff, parents, and communities.

50 Things You Can Do with Google Classroom
By Alice Keeler and Libbi Miller (@AliceKeeler, @MillerLibbi)

It can be challenging to add new technology to the classroom, but it's a must if students are going to be well-equipped for the future. Alice Keeler and Libbi Miller shorten the learning curve by providing a thorough overview of the Google Classroom App. Part of Google Apps for Education (GAfE), Google Classroom was specifically designed to help teachers save time by streamlining the process of going digital. Complete with screenshots, *50 Things You Can Do with Google Classroom* provides ideas and step-by-step instructions to help teachers implement this powerful tool.

50 Things to Go Further with Google Classroom
A Student-Centered Approach
By Alice Keeler and Libbi Miller (@AliceKeeler, @MillerLibbi)

Today's technology empowers educators to move away from the traditional classroom where teachers lead and students work independently—each doing the same thing. In *50 Things to Go Further with Google Classroom: A Student-Centered Approach*, authors and educators Alice Keeler and Libbi Miller offer inspiration and resources to help you create a digitally rich, engaging, student-centered environment. They show you how to tap into the power of individualized learning that is possible with Google Classroom.

Pure Genius

Building a Culture of Innovation and Taking 20% Time to the Next Level

By Don Wettrick (@DonWettrick)

For far too long, schools have been bastions of boredom, killers of creativity, and way too comfortable with compliance and conformity. In *Pure Genius*, Don Wettrick explains how collaboration—with experts, students, and other educators—can help you create interesting, and even life-changing, opportunities for learning. Wettrick's book inspires and equips educators with a systematic blueprint for teaching innovation in any school.

140 Twitter Tips for Educators

Get Connected, Grow Your Professional Learning Network, and Reinvigorate
Your Career

By Brad Currie, Billy Krakower, and Scott Rocco (@bradmcurrie, @wkrakower, @ScottRRocco)

Whatever questions you have about education or about how you can be even better at your job, you'll find ideas, resources, and a vibrant network of professionals ready to help you on Twitter. In *140 Twitter Tips for Educators,* #Satchat hosts and founders of Evolving Educators, Brad Currie, Billy Krakower, and Scott Rocco, offer step-by-step instructions to help you master the basics of Twitter, build an online following, and become a Twitter rock star.

Ditch That Textbook

Free Your Teaching and Revolutionize Your Classroom

By Matt Miller (@jmattmiller)

Textbooks are symbols of centuries-old education. They're often outdated as soon as they hit students' desks. Acting "by the textbook" implies compliance and a lack of creativity. It's time to ditch those textbooks—and those textbook assumptions about learning! In *Ditch That Textbook*, teacher and blogger Matt Miller encourages educators to throw out meaningless, pedestrian teaching and learning practices. He empowers them to evolve and improve on old, standard teaching methods. *Ditch That Textbook* is a support system, toolbox, and manifesto to help educators free their teaching and revolutionize their classrooms.

How Much Water Do We Have?

5 Success Principles for Conquering Any Challenge and Thriving in Times of Change

by Pete Nunweiler with Kris Nunweiler

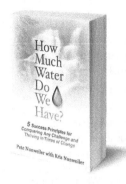

In *How Much Water Do We Have?* Pete Nunweiler identifies five key elements—information, planning, motivation, support, and leadership—that are necessary for the success of any goal, life transition, or challenge. Referring to these elements as the 5 Waters of Success, Pete explains that, like the water we drink, you need them to thrive in today's rapidly paced world. If you're feeling stressed out, overwhelmed, or uncertain at work or at home, pause and look for the signs of dehydration. Learn how to find, acquire, and use the 5 Waters of Success—so you can share them with your team and family members.

Instant Relevance

Using Today's Experiences to Teach Tomorrow's Lessons

By Denis Sheeran (@MathDenisNJ)

Every day, students in schools around the world ask the question, "When am I ever going to use this in real life?" In *Instant Relevance*, author and keynote speaker Denis Sheeran equips you to create engaging lessons *from* experiences and events that matter to your students. Learn how to help your students see meaningful connections between the real world and what they learn in the classroom—because that's when learning sticks.

The Classroom Chef

Sharpen Your Lessons. Season Your Classes. Make Math Meaningful.

By John Stevens and Matt Vaudrey (@Jstevens009, @MrVaudrey)

In *The Classroom Chef*, math teachers and instructional coaches John Stevens and Matt Vaudrey share their secret recipes, ingredients, and tips for serving up lessons that engage students and help them "get" math. You can use these ideas and methods as-is, or better yet, tweak them and create your own enticing educational meals. The message the authors share is that, with imagination and preparation, every teacher can be a classroom chef.

Start. Right. Now.

Teach and Lead for Excellence

By Todd Whitaker, Jeff Zoul, and Jimmy Casas
(@ToddWhitaker, @Jeff_Zoul, @casas_jimmy)

In their work leading up to *Start. Right. Now.*, Todd Whitaker, Jeff Zoul, and Jimmy Casas studied educators from across the nation and discovered four key behaviors of excellence: Excellent leaders and teachers *Know the Way, Show the Way, Go the Way, and Grow Each Day*. If you are ready to take the first step toward excellence, this motivating book will put you on the right path.

The Writing on the Classroom Wall

How Posting Your Most Passionate Beliefs about Education Can Empower Your Students, Propel Your Growth, and Lead to a Lifetime of Learning

By Steve Wyborney (@SteveWyborney)

In *The Writing on the Classroom Wall*, Steve Wyborney explains how posting and discussing Big Ideas can lead to deeper learning. You'll learn why sharing your ideas will sharpen and refine them. You'll also be encouraged to know that the Big Ideas you share don't have to be profound to make a profound impact on learning. In fact, Steve explains, it's okay if some of your ideas fall *off* the wall. What matters most is sharing them.

LAUNCH

Using Design Thinking to Boost Creativity and Bring Out the Maker in Every Student

By John Spencer and A.J. Juliani (@spencerideas, @ajjuliani)

Something happens in students when they define themselves as *makers* and *inventors* and *creators*. They discover powerful skills—problem-solving, critical thinking, and imagination—that will help them shape the world's future ... *our* future. In *LAUNCH*, John Spencer and A.J. Juliani provide a process that can be incorporated into every class at every grade level ... even if you don't consider yourself a "creative teacher." And if you dare to innovate and view creativity as an essential skill, you will empower your students to change the world—starting right now.

Kids Deserve It!

Pushing Boundaries and Challenging Conventional Thinking

By Todd Nesloney and Adam Welcome (@TechNinjaTodd, @awelcome)

In *Kids Deserve It!*, Todd and Adam encourage you to think big and make learning fun and meaningful for students. Their high-tech, high-touch, and highly engaging practices will inspire you to take risks, shake up the status quo, and be a champion for your students. While you're at it, you just might rediscover why you became an educator in the first place.

Escaping the School Leader's Dunk Tank

How to Prevail When Others Want to See You Drown

By Rebecca Coda and Rick Jetter (@RebeccaCoda, @RickJetter)

No school leader is immune to the effects of discrimination, bad politics, revenge, or ego-driven coworkers. These kinds of dunk-tank situations can make an educator's life miserable. By sharing real-life stories and insightful research, the authors (who are dunk-tank survivors themselves) equip school leaders with the practical knowledge and emotional tools necessary to survive and, better yet, avoid getting "dunked."

Teaching Math with Google Apps
50 G Suite Activities

By Alice Keeler and Diana Herrington (@AliceKeeler, @mathdiana)

Google Apps give teachers the opportunity to interact with students in a more meaningful way than ever before, while G Suite empowers students to be creative, critical thinkers who collaborate as they explore and learn. In *Teaching Math with Google Apps*, educators Alice Keeler and Diana Herrington demonstrate fifty different ways to bring math classes to the twenty-first century with easy-to-use technology.

Your School Rocks ... So Tell People!
Passionately Pitch and Promote the Positives Happening on Your Campus

By Ryan McLane and Eric Lowe (@McLane_Ryan, @EricLowe21)

Great things are happening in your school every day. The problem is, no one beyond your school walls knows about them. School principals Ryan McLane and Eric Lowe want to help you get the word out! In *Your School Rocks ... So Tell People!*, McLane and Lowe offer more than seventy immediately actionable tips along with easy-to-follow instructions and links to video tutorials. This practical guide will equip you to create an effective and manageable communication strategy using social media tools. Learn how to keep your students' families and community connected, informed, and excited about what's going on in your school.

Table Talk Math
A Practical Guide for Bringing Math into Everyday Conversations

By John Stevens (@Jstevens009)

Making math part of families' everyday conversations is a powerful way to help children and teens learn to love math. In *Table Talk Math*, John Stevens offers parents (and teachers!) ideas for initiating authentic, math-based conversations that will get kids to notice and be curious about all the numbers, patterns, and equations in the world around them.

Shattering the Perfect Teacher Myth
6 Truths That Will Help You THRIVE as an Educator

By Aaron Hogan (@aaron_hogan)

The idyllic myth of the perfect teacher perpetuates unrealistic expectations that erode self-confidence and set teachers up for failure. Author and educator Aaron Hogan is on a mission to shatter the myth of the perfect teacher by equipping educators with strategies that help them shift out of survival mode and THRIVE.

Shift This!

How to Implement Gradual Changes for MASSIVE Impact in Your Classroom

By Joy Kirr (@JoyKirr)

Establishing a student-led culture that isn't focused on grades and homework, but on individual responsibility and personalized learning may seem like a daunting task—especially if you think you have to do it all at once. But significant change is possible, sustainable, and even easy when it happens little by little. In *Shift This!* educator and speaker Joy Kirr explains how to make gradual shifts—in your thinking, teaching, and approach to classroom design—that will have a massive impact in your classroom. Make the first shift today!

Unmapped Potential

An Educator's Guide to Lasting Change

By Julie Hasson and Missy Lennard (@PPrincipals)

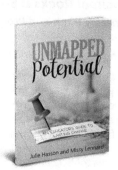

No matter where you are in your educational career, chances are you have, at times, felt overwhelmed and overworked. Maybe you feel that way right now. If so, you aren't alone. But the more important news is that things can get better! You simply need the right map to guide you from frustrated to fulfilled. *Unmapped Potential* offers advice and practical strategies to help you find your unique path to becoming the kind of educator—the kind of person—you want to be.

Social LEADia

Moving Students from Digital Citizenship to Digital Leadership

By Jennifer Casa-Todd (@JCasaTodd)

Equipping students for their future begins by helping them become digital leaders now. In our networked society, students need to learn how to leverage social media to connect to people, passions, and opportunities to grow and make a difference. *Social LEADia* addresses the need to shift the conversations at school and at home from digital citizenship to digital leadership.

Spark Learning

3 Keys to Embracing the Power of Student Curiosity

By Ramsey Musallam (@ramusallam)

Inspired by his popular TED Talk "3 Rules to Spark Learning," this book combines brain science research, proven teaching methods, and Ramsey's personal story to empower you to improve your students' learning experiences by inspiring inquiry and harnessing its benefits. If you want to engage students in more interesting and effective learning, this is the book for you.

Ditch That Homework
Practical Strategies to Help Make Homework Obsolete

By Matt Miller and Alice Keeler
(@jmattmiller, @alicekeeler)

In *Ditch That Homework*, Matt Miller and Alice Keeler discuss the pros and cons of homework, why teachers assign it, and what life could look like without it. As they evaluate the research and share parent and teacher insights, the authors offer a convincing case for ditching homework and replacing it with more effective and personalized learning methods.

The Four O'Clock Faculty
A Rogue Guide to Revolutionizing Professional Development

By Rich Czyz (@RACzyz)

Author Rich Czyz is on a mission to revolutionize professional learning for all educators. In *The Four O'Clock Faculty*, Rich identifies ways to make PD meaningful, efficient, and, above all, personally relevant. This book is a practical guide that reveals why some PD is so awful and what you can do to change the model for the betterment of you and your colleagues.

Culturize
Every Student. Every Day. Whatever It Takes.

By Jimmy Casas (@casas_jimmy)

In *Culturize*, author and education leader Jimmy Casas shares insights into what it takes to cultivate a community of learners who embody the innately human traits our world desperately needs, such as kindness, honesty, and compassion. His stories reveal how these "soft skills" can be honed while meeting and exceeding academic standards of twenty-first-century learning.

Code Breaker
Increase Creativity, Remix Assessment, and Develop a Class of Coder Ninjas!

By Brian Aspinall (@mraspinall)

Code Breaker equips you to use coding in your classroom to turn curriculum expectations into skills. Students learn how to identify problems, develop solutions, and use computational thinking to apply and demonstrate their learning. Best of all, you don't have to be a "computer geek" to empower your students with these essential skills.

The Wild Card

7 Steps to an Educator's Creative Breakthrough

By Hope and Wade King (@hopekingteach, @wadeking7)

Have you ever wished you were more creative . . . or that your students were more engaged in your lessons? *The Wild Card* is your step-by-step guide to experiencing a creative breakthrough in *your* classroom with your students. Wade and Hope King show you how to draw on your authentic self to deliver your content creatively and be the wild card who changes the game for your learners.

Stories from Webb

The Ideas, Passions, and Convictions of a Principal and His School Family

By Todd Nesloney (@TechNinjaTodd)

Stories from Webb goes right to the heart of education. Told by award-winning principal Todd Nesloney and his dedicated team of staff and teachers at Webb Elementary, this book will remind you why you became an educator. You'll be reinvigorated by these relatable stories—and you just may be inspired to tell your own!

The Principled Principal

10 Principles for Leading Exceptional Schools

By Jeffrey Zoul and Anthony McConnell (@Jeff_Zou, @mcconnellaw)

Jeffrey Zoul and Anthony McConnell know from personal experience that the role of school principal is one of the most challenging and the most rewarding in education. Using relatable stories and real-life examples, the authors reveal ten core values that will empower you to work and lead with excellence.

The Limitless School

Creative Ways to Solve the Culture Puzzle

By Abe Hege and Adam Dovico (@abehege, @adamdovico)

Culture is the invisible and driving force that shapes learning experiences, the community's perceptions, and students' memories—which is why being intentional about creating a positive culture is imperative for your school's success. This book identifies the nine pillars that support a positive school culture and explains how each stakeholder has a vital role to play in the work of making schools safe, inviting, and dynamic.

Google Apps for Littles

Believe They Can

By Christine Pinto and Alice Keeler (@pintobeanz11, @alicekeeler)

In *Google Apps for Littles*, author-educators Christine Pinto and Alice Keeler encourage teachers to tap into their young students' curiosity, particularly when it comes to technology. The authors share a wealth of innovative ways to integrate digital tools in the primary classroom to make learning engaging and relevant for even the youngest of today's twenty-first-century learners.

About the Authors

Marlena Hebern is known for her gentle approach to educators. She draws upon her eighteen years of successful classroom experience when training, supporting, and coaching teachers on engaging students through technology, hands on tech, and district implementation of technology programs.

After spending summers working at summer camps and as a swimming instructor, Marlena decided to pursue a career in education. Those early outdoor classroom experiences shaped her approach to education as she looked for ways to engage her students with hands on curriculum. Her greatest passion was teaching young children to read for the first time. (A thrill that will never grow old!)

Marlena also worked as an English language arts K–8 academic coach and as an English Language Arts K–8/English Language Learner Services Coordinator. She especially loves her current job as Coordinator II of Instructional Technology Services at Fresno County Superintendent of Schools in the California's Central Valley because she's in classrooms working with educators most of the time!

Marlena has been recognized as a Beginning Teacher Support Provider of the Year and has a master's degree in Reading Instruction. She is also a Google Certified Innovator, Google Certified Trainer, and co-founder of Edcamp Yosemite. Marlena also presents at local and regional conferences.

Marlena enjoys her rural home near Yosemite National Park and the outdoors with her husband, who is a talented (and retired) multimedia/video teacher. They are very proud of their two daughters, who are now embarking on their young careers, one as a Human Geographer and the other as an Aerospace Engineer.

Jon Corippo describes himself as a "formerly disgruntled student." He made it almost all the way through school at a 2.9 GPA. His final three semesters in advertising changed everything, though: Advertising classes were project based. Jon's grades shot to nearly 4.0. Also while at Fresno State, Jon served as a graduate assistant football coach, learning about leadership and teaching at the feet of Jim Sweeney. Jon graduated college with no intention of teaching.

After about seven years in non-educational jobs, Jon's amazing wife persuaded him to try his hand in education: He was hooked after just two days as a long-term sub on an emergency credential.

About twenty years later, Jon had served a decade at the K–8 level, opened a 1:1, project-based learning, Google-based high school, served in two county offices, including as an assistant superintendent and IT director. Jon has been recognized a County Teacher of the Year, a 20 to Watch Educator by the NSBA, and was a finalist in the EdTech Digest Awards. Jon also holds the Apple Distinguished Educator, Google Certified Innovator, and Microsoft Innovative Educator badges.

Jon is very proud of his work with CUE, where he currently serves as the organization's director. His work with CUE includes creating the CUE Rock Star concept of professional development, with a focus on hands-on learning and getting teachers connected via social media. CUE Rock Star Camps now include Admin, TOSA, Teacher and Specialized Editions for core areas. Jon has lead the development of the very successful CUE Launch program, and the well-received CUE BOLD Symposium. Under Jon's leadership, CUE professional learning has trained over 30,000 educators in only two years.

Jon lives in Coarsegold, California, near Yosemite, with his wife (a very successful educator), three children, and a random number of free-range chickens.

CPSIA information can be obtained
at www.ICGtesting.com
Printed in the USA
FFHW010835080619
52841025-58398FF

9 781946 444608